Through the pages of *Killing Christians* I have heard the command of Jesus reverberating through the martyrs' voices, "Deny yourself. Take up your cross. Follow Me." The men and women who have answered that summons—whose gripping stories Tom Doyle so movingly and powerfully shares in these pages—are my role models. They are authentic disciples. Their thrilling testimonies have put tears on my face, praise in my heart, fervency in my prayers, and renewed vigor to my steps as I, too, seek to follow Him.

—ANNE GRAHAM LOTZ
DAUGHTER OF BILLY GRAHAM
WWW.ANNEGRAHAMLOTZ.ORG

*Killing Christians* tells real-life stories of faith in action. These spiritual headlines from the persecuted church demonstrate there's another, deeper story unfolding behind the news of our day.

—CHRIS MITCHELL
CBN MIDDLE EAST BUREAU CHIEF
AND AUTHOR OF *DATELINE JERUSALEM*

It turns out that the "cloud of witnesses" mentioned in the book of Hebrews apparently have some kindred spirits modeling faithfulness right before our eyes today. If you are looking to be encouraged, challenged, and spurred on in your own life of faith pick up this book.

—TODD WAGNER
PASTOR OF WATERMARK CHURCH, DALLAS, TX

When I saw the title *Killing Christians* my heart sank and I wished that this book never had to be written. But then I read it. I felt like I was reading accounts from the Book of Acts. This is not about doom and despair, but about the "special grace" that Jesus gives to our brothers and sisters in the midst of suffering. You will be strengthened and blessed as you are moved to join hands with these strong followers of Jesus who stand for Him even in the face of prison or even death.

—ARTHUR BLESSITT
GUINNESS WORLD RECORD FOR CARRYING THE
CROSS IN EVERY NATION OF THE WORLD

As the twenty-first century unfolds, it is looking much like the first century for Christians. Persecution is everywhere. But, there are modern-day heroes of the faith who are showing us how we may all live hopefully and triumphantly for Christ even in the midst of extreme danger. *Killing Christians* will bless you and you will be encouraged to stand stronger in your own journey with Christ.

—CURTIS HAIL, PRESIDENT & CEO
E3 PARTNERS & I AM SECOND

*Killing Christians* is a penetrating look at what's happening on the front lines of the Church's greatest spiritual battle today. As in the first century, Christians are experiencing widespread persecution for their faith in Christ. Yet, the true stories in *Killing Christians* are miraculous accounts of God's faithfulness as believers live in the midst of ISIS, Hamas, The Brotherhood, and other terrorist regimes. Their stories will inspire you and refresh your faith!

—DR. CHARLIE DYER
PROFESSOR-AT-LARGE OF BIBLE AND HOST
OF *THE LAND AND THE BOOK* RADIO PROGRAM

Though today's headlines look grim, the resolve of the believers you meet in *Killing Christians* will inspire you and warm your heart. These true-life accounts take you to the front lines of the war that has been declared on Jesus' church. Yet in the midst of this war, the saints are shining brightly and their stories will thrill you! This book is awesome.

—RAY BENTLEY
PASTOR OF MARANATHA CHAPEL, SAN DIEGO, CA,
AND AUTHOR OF *THE HOLY LAND KEY*

There are more Christian martyrs today than at any other time in human history, which has been largely ignored by the press until recently. I am grateful that Tom has made known these remarkable stories of courage and conviction.

—DR. NEIL T. ANDERSON
FOUNDER AND PRESIDENT OF FREEDOM IN CHRIST
AND AUTHOR OF *THE BONDAGE BREAKER*

# KILLING CHRISTIANS

Living the Faith Where It's Not Safe to Believe

## TOM DOYLE
### with Greg Webster

W Publishing Group

An Imprint of Thomas Nelson

*To believers in prison, persecution, or danger*

Published in Nashville, Tennessee, by W Publishing Group, an imprint of Thomas Nelson.

Thomas Nelson titles may be purchased in bulk for educational, business, fund-raising, or sales promotional use. For information, please e-mail SpecialMarkets@ThomasNelson.com.

Library of Congress Control Number: 2014957694

ISBN 978-0-7180-3068-1

Printed in the United States of America

15 16 17 18 19 RRD 6 5 4 3 2 1

# CONTENTS

CONTENTS

# PREFACE

THE PEOPLE WHOSE stories you are about to read have endured the unendurable. Their suffering is so profound and their lives so worthy of respect that we want to be sure there is no mistaking the validity of what you read in these pages. In keeping with the gravity of the circumstances and with what the survivors still face, we've had to make a few changes.

The stories are not fiction. These are real people. While some stories involve the actual locations, others do not. But with every miracle, every answered prayer, every miraculous escape, as well as every bomb blast, each torture session, and each painful death, all occurred as recounted in these stories.

The narrative remains true to actual events, although we've at times modified such components as dialogue and physical descriptions. Each concluding message from a persecuted believer is presented in "writer's English" rather than in his or her own words, so nothing is lost in the translation.

Finally, as you read, please join us and pray for these new friends you are about to meet. Their lives are worthy of recognition, and their only request is that none of the glory would go to them as servants. That honor, of course, is reserved for their King alone.

Tom Doyle
Greg Webster
September 2014

# INTRODUCTION

*Persecution, the New Normal*

- Forty Egyptian churches burned to the ground
- House church leaders sentenced to Iran's infamous Evin prison
- Eighty Christians murdered in North Korea for merely owning a Bible
- Believers nailed to crosses in Syria

AND THAT'S THE news from just *one month* in 2014.

After that, it got really bad. In summer 2014, a shocked world witnessed the phenomenal rise of ISIS, now known as the Islamic State. Within weeks, a path of destruction swept through Syria and Iraq, leaving unimaginable carnage in its wake. The brutality of ISIS and its global jihadist agenda is reminiscent of the Assyrian Empire in the Old Testament. The Assyrians leveled villages and cities with such ferocity that, in the eighth century BC, the mere mention that Assyrians were on their way prompted some villages to commit mass suicide rather than be skinned alive, impaled, taken as slaves, or allow women to be abused and kidnapped. In a fascinating twist of history, ISIS was birthed in the same region as the Assyrians, and one of the organization's major objectives is now clear: to eradicate any presence of Christianity.

But ISIS is not alone in its quest against biblical faith. Christianity is under fire across the globe. Jesus lovers are hated in dozens of countries and often pay a gruesome price for following Him. Killing fields have become common, but this book isn't written to sound the alarm for the persecuted church. Others have already sent out the alert, and thankfully, many are listening. What the alarms can't tell you, though, is the inside human cost of following Jesus in the twenty-first century.

That's why these stories were written. It would be easy to conclude from the acceleration of Christian persecution that followers of Christ are on the run and are systematically being crushed by the forces of Islamic terrorism, fanatical dictators, and hostile nations. Yet the opposite is actually true.

Jesus said His followers would experience persecution *for merely being associated with Him.* He also predicted an escalation of intensity over time. On the night before He went to the cross, Jesus spelled out the details: "They will put you out of the synagogue: in fact, a time is coming when anyone who kills you will think he is offering a service to God" (John 16:2).

The evidence here suggests that the time Jesus referred to is *now*. In areas ripe with Muslim fundamentalism or controlled by sharia law, agreeing to return to Islam is the only way of escape for a believer with a knife to his or her throat. In places like Iran, only a full confession of apostasy, a complete list of names of underground house church leaders, and a reconversion to Islam can unlock the prison gate. In Mosul, Iraq, ISIS gave Christians four choices: *convert to Islam, pay a large and unaffordable jizya (tax), leave, or die.*

## THE NEW FACE OF CHRISTIANITY

OPPRESSORS OVER THE centuries have never recognized that the persecution of Christians is always a failed initiative. It just doesn't work. To the contrary, killing believers routinely *accelerates* the spread of the gospel and the growth of the church.

For those of us in the West, the threat of persecution is virtually nonexistent, but statistics show church growth in America—which experiences no persecution—has leveled off during the last twenty years. Why? Because Jesus' message of love and reconciliation thrives in a climate where hostility, danger, and martyrdom are present. Persecution and the spread of the gospel are as inseparable as identical twins. Suffering propels the growth of Jesus movements around the world.

So in Hamas-controlled Gaza, former Muslims worship Jesus right under the noses of terrorists. In Syria and Iraq, ISIS may grab headlines with beheadings and inhumane torture, but underground churches flourish. In Saudi Arabia, Muslims worship Jesus in Mecca and Medina, the heart of Islam.

As inconceivable as it is to Christians who have not faced life-threatening persecution, the suffering produces immense blessing through the radical transformation of individual believers. Each one comes away marked, never truly returning to the same life. Sometimes survivors are unrecognizable even by their own families because, in the midst of their brutal affliction, they experienced Christ in an hour of need as few of us ever do.

Persecuted believers have become the new face of *genuine* Christianity. They are filled with passion to live or die for Christ, and we in the West have much to learn from them.

The eight stories in this book introduce you to a handful of these courageous believers. They have learned to cling to Christ. Like a drowning man clutching a life preserver, it's just the believer and Jesus. And what have they discovered? That Jesus alone is always more than enough to take them by the hand through trial after life-threatening trial—not around the pain but all the way through.

Malik, a Christ follower from the Middle East, once told me: "Every Christian should go to jail at least once in life because of their faith in Christ. It's good for you!"

Can you relate to that? This former Muslim added: "You'll never be the same after experiencing the loneliness of a jail cell. But then there is great elation that comes when you realize Jesus is capable of filling 100 percent of that loneliness—and more. My deepest spiritual lessons were learned on the cold floor with no one there . . . but Jesus and me."

Malik is not alone in this conviction. A new generation has arrived. Widespread persecution can't stop the faithful who spread Jesus' love in the face of grave danger. Check out the news, and note the places where war, poverty, racism, seething religious violence, and killing seem to own the day. Right in the middle of it all, Jesus' church is thriving—thanks to people like those you'll meet in *Killing Christians*.

## A MESSAGE TO YOU

This book is about to take you on a journey to a place you've likely never been before: you're about to go underground. Jesus' church is there. While the world above ground often crumbles into chaos, Jesus' followers live on in peace and in the ultimate security of knowing Him.

A new Jesus movement is erupting around the world, and persecuted believers are leading the way. They have been given a gift from God that most of us would not want: the ability to endure enormous suffering and emerge even stronger. Church leaders in obscure places—outposts for the faith—are fully aware that passionately following Jesus has them on a collision course with hardship. They *will* be beaten, imprisoned, tortured, and maimed. Some will be killed. But unfazed, they move forward, in love with Jesus Christ.

Will persecution come to America? Maybe. If it does, remembering stories of those who have already endured and emerged faithful just may be a lifeline for you. And if persecution does not come upon the church in America, you may need these stories even more. They will inspire you to live with renewed passion for Jesus. For sure, you won't be able to read them and remain unmoved by these incredible, true accounts.

So, is Christianity winning or losing? This book is written to tell stories of victory from the front lines of a war raging around Jesus' church. The battle is fierce and not letting up.

Yet this is one of our finest hours.

# CHAPTER ONE

# THE PIRATES OF SOMALIA

A SOMALI STARED at the casket vibrating by his feet in the open bed of the truck as it juddered west toward Kenya. The left front tire dropped into a pothole and jolted a rifle from the man's lap. Grabbing the barrel, he steadied his weapon, sneered, and rolled his head away from the cargo. Turning was pointless, of course. Stench from the decomposing body in the container enshrouded the vehicle, but the evasive movement helped the man feel a measure of control over his dismal mission. He wondered how he would endure the hours-long drive that remained. Perhaps a stop for noon prayers would help. He scowled back at the man-sized box.

*Inside* the coffin, Azzam Azziz Mubarak stifled a retch. The three-day-old corpse on top of him pressed breath from the stowaway's lungs. Inhaling required not only physical exertion but mental resolve to convince the nostrils that taking in the putrefied air was necessary. Threads of the burial cloth peeled off Azzam's sweat-drenched cheek as he turned his head in an effort to find more breathing room. He shifted his left leg, the one body part not covered with a dead man. Regardless of the inconvenience the deceased had undoubtedly endured in life, Azzam was thankful that the corpse's missing leg, which would have lain on top of him, now gave him a spot of relief from the crushing weight.

*I will suffocate before we even get to the checkpoint,* Azzam thought.

The living man in the box struggled to raise his head to the top of the casket. With the back of his skull pressed against the end to support his weight—and that of the body on top of him—he pushed his right index finger up against the cover and raised it an inch. Azzam winced as daylight blasted through the gap. He squinted toward the guard, who was busy resettling the gun in his lap. The man checked to make sure the safety was on, then twisted his head away from the truck bed and spoke to the driver at his back. Azzam made out the words "noon" and "prayers." The driver nodded, and the truck swerved to the side of the road and jerked to a stop.

Azzam silently lowered the coffin cover. The truck rocked as its guard scrambled over the side. Azzam heard the driver's door slam shut and listened to their conversation fade as the two men walked toward a cluster of shacks about a hundred yards to the right of where they had parked.

Once both men were gone, Azzam freed his arms, torso,

and head from the dead man's weight, propped himself on his right elbow and pushed up the casket lid with his left hand. He stretched his head into the open air. Compared to the stench he'd been breathing for the past several hours, the outside air felt like a fresh mountain breeze. He even noticed the fragrance of bread baking over an open fire next to one of the distant shacks. Food would be wonderful, but for now that was impossible.

His thoughts shifted to the prospect of escape. Should he make a run for it? No; he instantly brushed aside the idea—he still had too far to go. Even by truck, it would be nightfall before he made it to Kenya.

Azzam leaned back in the coffin, the lid still raised to let in as much air as possible, while keeping an eye on the shacks to watch for the return of his chauffeurs. In the relative comfort of his half-sitting position, he mused over this bizarre situation. What a crazy world, that he is safest traveling in a coffin under a corpse. The preferred transportation system for the underground network of Bible smugglers, it was a magnificently strange way to put Muslim drivers to work for the gospel. No follower of Allah would dare open a casket, let alone look beneath the remains. Although touching the dead was not specifically forbidden, superstition runs strong among Somali Muslims, and dead bodies were kept as far away as possible.

Under dead people, Bibles could get to believers and saints in Somalia, and endangered believers and saints (as if they weren't *all* endangered!) could get out to Kenya. Not once had anyone been caught. But more than a few times when the coffin reached its destination, there had been two corpses inside.

Azzam assured himself he would not be one on this trip—or on his return to Somalia in a week or so with more Bibles.

Azzam heard the men arguing before he saw them round the closest shack to the truck. He couldn't tell what had upset them, but he took one last breath of fresh air and ducked again into the darkness of the casket, still musing over how his lot in life had come to this.

A few months earlier, Azzam had needed spiritual guidance.

"The man you see in your dreams is the devil. Don't listen to him!"

Azzam stood silently as Imam Hussein Mohammad berated him. In a harangue that lasted several minutes, the village spiritual master reviled Azzam and his story in every way possible.

"These visions—or whatever you call them—are false. Every one of them! I hear this all the time. Do not be one of the deceived ones. When you have a dream of the Great Prophet, come see me."

"But I've had *seven* visions about the man who calls Himself Jesus. Why do I keep having them? What is He trying to tell me?"

A backhand to Azzam's face answered his questions. The blow from the village imam hurled Azzam onto his back in a pile of shoes left by the faithful at the mosque entrance. The cleric glared fire at the dazed inquirer on the floor. Friday prayers occupied the throngs inside the sacred building, and no one noticed the semiconscious man lying among their shoes.

Prayers droned in Azzam's thickened brain. He lay motionless, eyes shut, until Imam Hussein turned and joined the faithful in prayer. Still dazed, Azzam rose to his hands and knees and crawled out the doorway. *What if I'd told him the last time I saw Jesus was in this very mosque?* Azzam wondered as he pulled himself to his feet and stepped into the sunlight to begin a slow walk home. *I'd probably be dead.*

Azzam plodded into his room. His plan to throw himself onto his bed for the rest of the afternoon was cut short by the sight. He leaned his shoulder against the doorframe and stared at the object in his bed. "How can this be?" he whispered to himself. The wooden cross was three feet long and drenched in blood.

"Who put that in here? Someone set me up. If father saw this, he would . . . If *anyone* saw this . . ."

"*My blood is still fresh enough for you, Azzam!*" Azzam startled at the words from nowhere. He glanced up and around the room. Jesus' voice—he had heard it enough by now to recognize it immediately—was loud enough to be heard anywhere in the house. Azzam looked again at his bed, now covered in blood.

The shock of the vision finally brought Azzam fully alert. He raced out of the room and grabbed his mother, who stood, otherwise undisturbed, in the kitchen. He pulled her to his room, his younger brother, Hajj, following close behind.

"Mother! Who put the cross on my bed?"

"What cross? Azzam, have you lost your mind? There's nothing on your bed." She pointed toward the mattress. "But what's the smell of blood in here? Did you get into *another* fight? Have you finally killed someone?"

Though two years younger than Azzam, Hajj was already a powerful young man. He grabbed Azzam's shirt and threw him to the floor. With his bare foot, he kicked Azzam in the face. Hajj sneered at his spiritually deviant older brother and huffed as he left the room. He would find their father and tell him everything.

Alone with his mother, Azzam pleaded, "Mother, Jesus was here—again! You believe me, don't you? You have to. Why would I make this up? Didn't you hear Him?"

Rawia Mubarak looked her oldest child calmly in the eye. "Leave, son, and don't come back."


Azzam had walked, almost without stopping, the twenty-five miles to a village where he knew friends would protect him. He arrived well past midnight on the day after the cross had appeared on his bed. Now, after three weeks in hiding, Azzam felt certain his father had a general idea of where he was, but Azzam was wrong; his father knew *exactly* where he was hiding. A warlord and pirate as effective as the senior Mubarak knew the whereabouts of any person of interest within his domain.

"Package for Azzam Mubarak!" A man shouted from just outside the safe house.

Azzam appeared in the doorway. The deliveryman lowered his voice and said gravely, "It's from your father."

Azzam stared through the man, then fixed his eyes on the package the stranger had placed on the ground. The man stepped back from the parcel as Azzam spoke, only half addressing the courier. "My father? Why?"

Azzam scanned nearby houses. The village seemed unusually quiet. No one was on the street. Was this a setup? A bomb in the package? Would pirates move in for the kill as soon as its recipient picked up the box?

Azzam blinked three times as possibilities raced through his mind. *Or has my father had a change of heart? Maybe this is a peace offering. He once told me I was the next in line. Perhaps he is giving me a second chance.* Azzam had already proven himself as a pirate. His father should welcome him in his footsteps as a warlord.

The deliveryman backed further away as Azzam approached the package. Azzam knelt, placed a hand on each side of the box, and rocked gently. The weight felt strange but lacked the mechanical quality he would expect from a threatening device. He peeled open the stout box.

Nothing he had imagined prepared Azzam for the contents. His head jerked involuntarily away from the sight. Inside a clear plastic bag, human body parts formed a gooey mass of red tissue and brown flesh. It was his mother.

Retaliation was standard operating procedure among Somali warlords, but that his father would butcher his mother because she helped him escape had been unthinkable even to a young man steeped in the often-grisly profession of piracy. As if to emphasize the unfeeling execution, a photograph had been laid atop the bag of human remains. It showed his mother kneeling in front of two men Azzam recognized, their knives raised over the tearful woman. So, Mahdi and Yasin had been the designated killers. They had done their job well.

Across the bottom of the photo in his father's handwriting

was a message for Azzam: "If you try to bury your mother in Somalia, we will dig her up and feed her to dogs."

The next day, Azzam carted his mother's body to the coast and buried her at sea.


Oval. Three. Right. Slash.

Azzam Mubarak's life as a pirate ended the day he opened the package from his father, and shortly after, his life as a bold follower of the One he now knew to be more than just a Great Prophet began. The courageous son of a warlord strode with purpose down the middle of the dusty village road. A dozen eyes read his hand signals but none acknowledged.

Fifteen minutes later, twelve people gathered furtively in one of the village homes. Three knocked, in turn, at the back door. Several others scrambled through a window on the north side of the house. The rest crawled through the south-facing window. No one entered by the front door. This was the second meeting of Somali believers in the village ten miles south of Mogadishu. Until two months earlier, the population had been 100 percent Muslim.

Now the group leader, Azzam spent many nights wide-awake in candlelight meetings—answering questions and telling the story of a mysterious, bloody cross in his bedroom. After the first meeting, the Jesus followers had paid a staggering price. Azzam survived, but six were executed the week after they met. They had been dragged from their mud-and-dung homes in the middle of the night and decapitated. The foregone sentences were announced and carried out so the whole village could hear each gruesome killing. It was meant to end any future conversions. Jesus was not welcome here.

*But He came back anyway.*

Twelve new followers sat in silence as Azzam reviewed the hand signals. "Oval means *meeting*. Three is for the *third house*. Right is the *direction*. Slash means *as soon as you can*."

Then he opened the only Bible in the village—most likely the only one in the entire province. "Blessed are the poor in spirit," he read, "for theirs is the kingdom of heaven. Blessed are those who mourn, for they will be comforted" (Matt. 5:3–4).

Family members of the recently departed smiled. They mourned but wanted the joy their loved ones had possessed, even if it meant they would experience it here on earth for only a short time. The group sat in silence for several minutes.

Jabar interrupted the quiet. "Azzam, why did your mom order you to leave? Couldn't you have stood up to her?"

Azzam had not yet told this new group his whole story. He looked intently at the new follower. "That's the old way, Jabar. I knew I had to leave. For my father—you know him—business rules his life. A warlord who controls as much as he does could not afford to have a Jesus follower as a son. He would not have killed me himself, but I would be dead nonetheless. He would have sent his pirates, who would do the job without a second thought. It's their duty, their *religion*. My mother knew that, too, and wanted only to save me. They're still looking for me and won't give up—*halal*,* you know. When my mother ordered me to leave, it was the last time I ever saw her."

Then he told a stunned assembly about the package.

"But we have each other. You are my family now. Jesus called each one of us, just like a shepherd calls his sheep. You know how it is. You heard His voice—some of you literally—and answered the call. Remember: Jesus told us, 'Brother will betray brother to death, and a father his child'" (Matt. 10:21).

Unwilling to leave the group morosely pondering his story, Azzam changed the subject. "Tomorrow, I'll be leaving the country."

"What? But why?" Jabar yelled. The others winced, and several hands reached to cover the mouth of the man who had spoken too loudly.

Azzam put a finger to his lips. Only a quiet meeting could be a safe meeting. "The enemy prowls. He's tightening his grip like a hangman's noose around the neck. But we are not criminals. We've been set free. Jesus does not condemn us. Only those who hate Him do.

"I'm going to Kenya. They have Bibles there. Believers who want to give them to us have contacted me." He paused and scanned the group. "My trip will take about a week, maybe more. But when I come back, each of you will have a small copy of the Scriptures—small enough to hide easily.

"We must arm ourselves with the Word. You'll memorize as much as you can and then pass the Bibles along to others who

---

* A reference to something permissible by Islamic law, such as an honor killing.

are also waiting for them. We must get stronger because our battle is only going to get worse. Much worse."

Jabar looked sadly at Azzam. "You'll be dead before you reach the border," he whispered.

"Maybe, Jabar, but I have a plan."

The truck jolted back onto the road and resumed its journey toward Kenya. *So far the plan has worked perfectly.* Azzam smiled and settled under the dead body as it jiggled west.

Two weeks and a second trip under a corpse later, Azzam was home.

Oval. Seven. Left. Slash.

This time, it was Jabar who walked the village road, signaling. He resisted a smile. Within minutes, twelve believers sat on the floor of a new meeting place. They prayed passionately for an hour. Many offered prayers for Azzam's safety.

A sound at the back door halted the prayers. Eyes opened, wondering what would happen next. The door opened slowly, and Azzam stepped into the room and set a box on the floor. A dozen pairs of relieved and grateful arms rushed to embrace their returning leader.

"The Bibles are well-worn. Our Kenyan brothers and sisters have read them for years. You should have seen their joy as they gave them to me. They send them with their love."

For another hour, prayers and tears of joy anointed each

copy. Finally, Azzam brought the meeting to a close. They had stayed together a dangerously long time. One at a time, the twelve believers slipped out of the house.

Two men strolled arrogantly down the center of the village road. Preoccupied over boasting about exploits with their latest girlfriends, they didn't notice a third man step silently from between two houses and into the road a dozen yards ahead of them. Their banter stopped abruptly as Mahdi and Yasin recognized the form in their path. They were not at all happy to see Azzam Mubarak again.

"I know what you did to my mother."

"Azzam, we had to. We didn't want to do it, but your father ordered us and threatened to . . ." As he spoke, Mahdi's right hand moved slowly around his back.

"I know all about my father." Azzam stared at the two murderers. "I haven't come to harm you." He paused for effect. "I've come to forgive you."

Mahdi and Yasin glanced sideways at each other and then back at the man facing them, wondering whether or not to believe the words they had just heard.

Azzam continued, "You need to know that I love you and have prayed for both of you ever since I saw your picture with my mother. Jesus filled my heart with compassion for you. You need Him—just like I did. He can forgive murderers. His love is greater than anything you've done."

It was the first meeting between the three men. They met

again—at night—several more times. Impelled by Azzam's testimony, Mahdi and Yasin offered their lives of piracy to a forgiving Savior. For the moment, the two new believers and Azzam told no one else what had happened.

Afternoon hand signals directed group members to come together hours later for a midnight gathering. Concern that meetings held immediately after the signaling might be garnering suspicion prompted delays in the group's start times. All were present before Azzam arrived.

Jabar gasped and felt instantly light-headed as the group leader walked in the *front* door. Every conversation in the room stopped mid-sentence. Behind Azzam Mubarak stood Mahdi and Yasin.

Azzam returned the dozen troubled gazes. He lifted his left hand toward the two men in the doorway. "Mahdi and Yasin are part of the family now. They are forgiven."

A smile spread slowly across Azzam's face as he let the words sink in. No one else spoke. The same questions played in the minds of all the believers in the room: how could Azzam be smiling at men who had butchered his mother? How could he even stand in their presence? Some sort of vengeance must be in his heart.

Mahdi broke the silence. "In my religion, there was no certainty of forgiveness—either from God or each other. When Yasin and I saw Azzam on the road last week, I reached for my knife, assuming I would need to defend myself. There would be no other reason for him to confront us other than to avenge his mother's death and kill us both to honor her.

"But when Azzam spoke, his words paralyzed both of us. We could not believe what we were hearing. His words of forgiveness . . . I had never heard anything like it."

Mahdi paused and looked at the floor. Then, eyeing the group, he continued, "I have longed for words like this often during my life. For Azzam to forgive murderers like us and to tell us that he loves us . . . is . . . unbelievable." Mahdi hung his head.

Yasin picked up the story. "For the last week, all three of us have been meeting at night. Azzam has shown us that Jesus can forgive the worst of sinners. Moses killed a man, and Paul ordered people to their deaths. But they, too, were forgiven and redirected. This is still hard for us to believe; yet we know it's true.

"Jesus has even forgiven us for being pirates. Stealing and killing was our way of life. Only Jesus could forgive us, and only Jesus could give Azzam the heart to forgive us. Mahdi and I . . . we are believers now. So there is peace between us, between Azzam and us. And you all."

Yasin looked at Mahdi, who added, "We've also seen that Jesus has given brother Azzam unusual insight. He's able to see things the Lord reveals to him."

Jabar's eyes widened as Mahdi put his around Azzam.

"Azzam knew something didn't add up until Yasin and I told him more about his mother's death. Azzam had hoped, deep in his heart, something about his mother that he just had to know—and he was right. As we killed her, her last words were: 'Jesus, Jesus, I love You.'"

## A MESSAGE FROM AZZAM

My life in Christ has never long been free from severe testing and difficult trials. But in the midst of them, I have seen His power. Eventually, I found out that my mother was having dreams about Jesus at the same time I was. Earlier in her life, she had met a missionary who taught her about the Bible, and the stories and Scripture verses never left her heart.

If I could ask her one question, it would be: "Mother did you see the cross on my bed that day, too?" She never said. She just told me to go because she feared for my life.

I discipled Mahdi and Yasin, and both have joined the underground work of the Lord. Only the gracious Lord Jesus could have taken the all-consuming anger, rage, and hatred for them out of my heart.

I have been a believer now for fifteen years. When I married, my wife knew we would not have a normal life. She told me, "Azzam, we will live in danger until the day we die as martyrs for Christ, but I will walk this journey with you joyfully."

*Die as martyrs for Christ!* What a fearless woman of God! I am beyond blessed to have her as my partner in life.

Our son Hakeem has been kidnapped three times by pirates.

They attempt to brainwash young boys and commit them to pirating for life, but each time they've tried with Hakeem, God has been gracious to restore our son.

While people ordinarily travel on foot, on a donkey, or by bus, I'm still riding in caskets. It's the only way to get Bibles spread around to the saints. I love the irony that caskets for dead people are used by God to bring new life into Somalia! Underground believers—and there are many now—are being transformed into the likeness of our Savior through this Book.

As a pirate, I was a risk taker, and that has not changed since I became a missionary in the underground. The Horn of Africa is an evil place. Satan has a stronghold on families, government, education, and of course, Islam. The devil fights us at every turn, but God has the upper hand in the way He uses any harm thrown at us by demonic powers.

*Patience* is a spiritual fruit I have learned with difficulty but value deeply. When you are a risk taker, it's easy to charge ahead and take all matters into your own hands, but that often is not God's way. Jesus put me "in school" to learn to wait upon Him.

Through trials, God has taught me patience. Trials line up to test us. Just as we are finished with one, another is waiting for us.

But trials are also a Holy Place for the believer. They force us to pull away and get on our faces before God. In a trial, it's just Jesus and you. Psalm 23:4 says: "I walk through the valley of the shadow of death." You eventually emerge from a trial, but that time spent with Christ will have marked you, and you will be different, forever. No matter how bad it gets, you reap the rewards of faithfulness if you stay the course.

When a believer suffers, he or she is like an Old Testament high priest in the Holy of Holies. Although our human tendency is to move quickly, this is not a time to rush. The Old Testament priest performed his duties meticulously because the opportunity came just once a year. Not only was every second of the time sacred, but the one chosen to act as high priest knew it was a great honor to offer this sacrifice for the living God.

That's how we should be—patient with the calling on our lives and honored to perform the sacrifice of self for God. Time with Christ in tribulation is a sacred, divinely arranged service in the Holy of Holies. When it comes to you, consider it an honor to have been selected. Don't rush. Wait for the Lord. He is there with you, just as He was with David when he wrote these majestic words: "I will fear no evil, for You are with me" (v. 5). Can you be in a better place?

Remember us here in Somalia in your prayers. We send our love in Christ.

# CHAPTER TWO

# THE ONLY EMPTY GRAVEYARD IN SYRIA

A HOT, LATE-AFTERNOON breeze rustled palm fronds on the trees standing watch over six thousand empty seats in the world's largest restaurant. Thirty feet below, the establishment's signature fountain, a misty, liquid dandelion the height of a grown man, radiated feathery sprays of water into its pool set among the barren tables. A line of eight short, vertical spouts marched north from the dandelion, parading in front of no one. Where thousands of diners should be glutting themselves on delights from India, China, Saudi Arabia, Iran, and other wedges of the Middle East, no more than thirty patrons resolutely consumed their food.

Above the tranquilizing swoosh of the fountains, indistinct voices of the few restaurant staff still on duty echoed from the adjacent indoor sections. Within the tunnel-shaped interior, table lamps cast spots of romance on sandstone ceilings, tan light wasting its effect for want of lovers to appreciate the mood. In the massive kitchen, half the size of an American grocery store, a handful of chefs with little to do wandered among vacant ovens and abandoned cooking surfaces where several hundred food preparers would be working on a more typical day. Just outside of the main kitchen door, the jangle of a lone plate dropping on tile echoed across nearly five acres of seating and momentarily interrupted the conversation of two men.

Farid Assad glanced back from the direction of the sound and smiled as he dipped hot pita bread into a fresh bowl of hummus. He placed the morsel reverently between his lips and, savoring the taste, pointed over his companion's shoulder at the twenty-foot-tall sign declaring the Damascus Gate Restaurant the holder of a Guinness world record.

"This is nothing but our usual hangout, and as many times as we eat here, it still amuses me that people come from all over the planet just to say they've had a meal at the world's largest restaurant. Here in Damascus! How strange is that?"

Farid paused as he swirled another piece of bread in the bowl. "Joseph, I've never seen so few people here. By rights, I suppose *no one* should be here—probably not even us. Last week, the fighting was just down the street."

Pastor Joseph's eyes scanned the rows of empty tables. He was used to being wary of people around them, but today there were obviously no threats nearby. The danger lay outside, where the latest assault by the Free Syrian Army was in full swing.

Joseph smirked as he looked back at his friend on the other side of the table.

"You're the one who should worry," he chuckled. "With the last name Assad, you could get killed by any of the terrorist groups vying for Damascus just by introducing yourself."

Farid returned the smirk and nodded at the unpleasant truth. *Assad* was a common, if unpopular, name these days. The Alawite president of Syria, Bashar al-Assad, had mobilized Syria's army several months ago to fortify the capital city, but now rebel forces took it from their hated enemy street by street. The Free Syrian Army led the way.

If there was a blessing in the madness, it was that the Sunni Muslim front was badly fractured. When terrorist gangs weren't dispensing violence within sight of government buildings, they busied themselves killing each other as they competed for ultimate control of the Arab world.

Farid finished the appetizer, pointed at his plate, and motioned to a waiter who had nothing better to do than watch his two customers' every move. The server understood and headed to the kitchen to fetch more food.

"Joseph, you heard about the soldiers from Iran, didn't you? Tehran sent a whole new unit just this week."

The pastor blew air through closed lips and shook his head. He hadn't heard the news.

"I hear that President Assad and the Ayatollah are getting nervous—with good reason. Now that the sanctions are lifted, Iran will have enough money to keep this proxy war of theirs going for years."

Joseph cut in, "And our other Arab 'friends' can supply the *Sunni* front for just as long. Word on the street is that the Sunnis will outlast the Alawites. Now the chances are even better with Iran dogging the president as well."

Farid looked away from his companion and stared for a few seconds down the line of fountains before speaking again. "Do you believe the Isaiah prophecy has been fulfilled?" Farid turned back toward his spiritual mentor and noticed their waiter, a dozen tables away, returning from the kitchen with kabobs.

Farid's question was likely the most talked-about theological topic among Damascus Christians these days. Pastor Joseph sat back in his chair and folded his arms, considering how to answer. "'Look, Damascus is no longer a city'" (HCSB). He whispered the key phrase from Isaiah 17:1. "To tell you the truth, I'm not sure anymore. But if Damascus is still to be leveled, how ironic would it be that Arabs may do the leveling!"

A head-splitting blast punctuated Pastor Joseph's sentence. He lurched forward as water sloshed over the sides of the fountain pools. The approaching waiter stumbled into a chair, and skewers splattered across several tables. Farid gripped the edge of his table and slid out of the seat and onto his knees, crouching for cover. Screams of other diners meshed with reverberations from the explosion. Joseph pitched himself to the floor.

The restaurant lights flickered off as stunned customers huddled breathless under their tables. Screams erupted again as three more explosions in rapid succession somewhere outside rattled several hundred dishes off of shelves. The crackle of shattering dinnerware matched the intensity of the bomb blasts.

Farid and Joseph winced, jerking their hands up to cover their ears. Beige clouds of smoke and dirt billowed over the walls and into the open-air dining room. Just up the Damascus Airport Motorway from the giant restaurant, where several hundred FSA soldiers advanced toward the international airport, Syrian artillery had begun the counteroffensive.

Inside the Damascus Gate Restaurant, fountains hissed eerily in the otherwise silent aftermath of the exploding ordnance. Farid squinted through tan dust settling over the world-famous eatery.

"Joseph, are you all right?"

"I suppose," the other man responded, half under the table and resting on his hands and knees. Straightening his torso, Joseph plopped his left arm on the table and looked at his friend. "I also suppose you were right. We shouldn't have come here today. I guess we're blessed, though. This could have been much worse."

"And still might be." Farid watched dust-speckled men and women, recovering their senses, as they began picking their way through bronze fog toward the exits. "We need to go."

Joseph nodded and stood up.

The Damascus Gate Restaurant, which prided itself on staying open seven days a week, would be closing early today. As Farid and Joseph hustled toward the nearest door, Farid noticed Shaker Al Samman, the owner, standing by a waiter station ringed with a pile of broken dishes, watching the few customers leave his restaurant. The businessman with his head and tailored suit coated with tan sprinkles, reminded Farid of one of the restaurant's featured desserts, topped with powdered sugar.

Farid angled toward Al Samman while fishing in his pocket for a few Syrian pounds, but Shaker waved him off. "Don't bother," he called to the regular guest. "Just come back sometime when it's safe—whenever that may be!"

Farid and Joseph nodded simultaneously and resumed their trek toward the exit. Most of their fellow patrons had scattered by the time the two men reached the curb outside the restaurant. Although they saw no evidence of troops nearby, neither was there any evidence of taxi activity. Apparently, most of the other customers lived nearby and were heading home on foot, but distance rendered that not an option for Farid and Joseph. The friends scanned the roadway within view, wondering what to do next.

Ten minutes into their hope for a taxi, the sun dipped below the rooftops of the Old City of Damascus. Traffic streamed away from the airport—delivery trucks, motorcycles, private cars, but no taxis.

Farid finally broke the silence between the two worried figures at the curbside. "What? Did every cab in town get advanced word of the attack and stay away from the airport?"

Joseph and Farid ducked involuntarily as multiple explosions—all farther away than the ones that had interrupted their dinner—flashed in the twilight.

Righting himself, Farid raised his hands in the direction of the blasts and grumbled, "Maybe the Damascus prophecy will be fulfilled while we wait for a taxi."

Suddenly, Joseph slapped Farid's right shoulder with the back of his left hand and pointed past his friend. A gray Hyundai

Elantra screeched to the curb less than a yard from Farid. As a man inside flung open the passenger side door, Farid stepped back. He counted ten bullet holes in the open door.

"Get in!"

Joseph recognized Hanna Tarazi as his friend, stretched across the front seat from the driver's side, motioned them to the car.

"Are you the only two people in the city who didn't know the war was coming this way tonight?"

Farid and Joseph scrambled into the car, and Hanna gunned away from the sidewalk before the passengers had even shut their doors.

"Hanna, my friend!" Farid settled into the backseat. "How did you know we were here?"

"I didn't. I spotted you from two blocks away. I couldn't believe you would be standing right out there in the open! You have got to be more careful! This is not the place to be hanging out right now."

"Well, I'm glad you saw us." Joseph rested his arm across the space between the two front seats, his left hand nearly touching Hanna's shoulder. "The cabs knew enough not to be anywhere near."

Hanna seemed not to hear Joseph's comment. He glanced in the rearview mirror, then turned his head enough to see both passengers out of the corner of his eye.

"They have chemical weapons again." He grimaced. "Both sides! I heard they've already been used. The Sunnis will let them loose on their own people. After all, what do the lives of a few hundred matter when you can hang the bad press on Bashar al-Assad, right? How sick this war is!"

"Hanna, how have *you* survived?" Joseph looked hard at his friend. "Your family home is right in the eye of the storm."

"It hasn't been easy; believe me. Did you check out the new decorations on my car? I drove right into a gunfight and got it from both sides. I stopped at a light, and the shooting started so fast I could only duck and pray. The right side is Alawite, and the left is compliments of al-Qaeda."

He stared back at the road.

"I wonder if my family can dare to live here anymore." The driver tossed a hand in the air. "Not that we'd have a place to go." Hanna stopped his monologue and glanced again at his passengers. "Where are you staying tonight?"

"I was hoping to stay in Damascus with Joseph and head up north tomorrow." Farid leaned forward against the back of Joseph's seat. "But his house is in *your* neighborhood. Not exactly a peaceful night's rest. This is going to be a long night. With all the shooting and bombs, we really should go north right away. "

"Great!" Hanna's reply startled Farid. "I'll take you. It's going to require some fancy maneuvering to get through the checkpoints. I'm not even sure they'll be open. We seem to have reached another flash point in Syria, haven't we?" He stared soberly out the windshield and said softly, "Our country is unraveling."

The three men rode in silence for several minutes before Hanna picked up the conversation again.

"We do need to get each other caught up on the latest about all our new friends. My living room has seen many joyful visitors

lately. The worship is especially sweet in the middle of the night."
He smiled at Pastor Joseph. "*Jesus* hasn't given up on Syria!"

Three hours later, the Hyundai was still weaving the
streets of Damascus. Bombed out roads, risky checkpoints, and
detours to avoid advancing terrorist factions left no direct route
out of the city. The three men had ridden in tense silence for
the past hour, and they all flinched at the bleep of Hanna's cell
phone.

"Habibi! Where are you meeting?" Hanna paused for the
answer. "Just north of Damascus at midnight? Yes. We should
be able to make it!"

Hanna touched the phone with his thumb to end the call
and grinned at his companions. "Well, friends, it seems we will
stay near Damascus tonight after all. We've been summoned to
a meeting. That's all I can tell you at the moment except that I
can also say the northern area appears to be quiet tonight. We
should be okay."

At 12:15, the car pulled up to a dark house in a northern suburb
of the Syrian capital. Hanna turned to Farid and Joseph and
motioned for quiet. They closed car doors softly behind them
and walked silently to the unlit entrance of the house. Hanna
motioned for his friends to follow him inside as he turned the
knob and slid open the front door.

Drawn curtains eliminated even the ambient light from
outside, and the three men stepped into a black interior. Farid
and Joseph stopped and listened as Hanna shuffled forward in

the darkness. When their eyes adjusted, they saw that the room was not completely lightless. A sliver glowed under the crack of a door. The silhouette of Hanna's legs moved in front of the strip of light, and they heard the turning of a doorknob. A golden glow spread into the room, revealing a stairway leading below.

The three men ambled down a flight of stairs, obviously taking them to a basement and into stronger light. Hanna opened a door at the bottom of the steps. Brightness and sound washed over the three men, and Farid and Joseph could hardly believe what they saw from the doorway. Thirty or more people stood almost shoulder to shoulder, many of them with hands raised in worship. Their singing was electrifying. Farid wondered what sort of sound insulation had kept the magnificent chorus from being heard outside.

Stepping into the room, Joseph patted Farid's shoulder and pointed at several people. Farid's eyes widened, and he nodded slowly, amazed at what he saw. Both Sunnis and Alawites—all former enemies—stood together. Some rested loving hands on each other's shoulders. Most nodded together with the music. All smiled broadly.

In the streets just south of the house, Sunnis and Alawites were spending this night shooting each other. Here, they joined one another in worship of the Savior they now had in common.

Joseph leaned forward and whispered in Farid's ear, "I feel honored to be here."

Farid nodded. Both men felt the enormous gravity of this event. In nearby parts of Damascus, both sides were hell-bent on destroying each other. But that was hell. This was heaven.

Two hundred miles north, a steel-eyed, twentysomething Sunni man pressed the muzzle of a semiautomatic pistol into the side of Haytham Assad's head. Farid's father was surprised at the early arrival of the two terrorists. They were ahead of the larger pack. *Probably trying to earn their share of virgin-points before more experienced jihadists can take the glory.* The older man sat frozen, guessing the worst of his visitors' intentions.

"I don't have any money to give you and wouldn't even if I did. I'm a pastor."

"Your Jesus is weak." Perspiration trickled down the right side of the intruder's light-brown face. "We need to teach you and your Christian friends a lesson."

Suhad Assad sat on the floor in the corner of the couple's living room and wept quietly. She knew that five neighbors had been killed in the apartment building that morning, and she feared irritating the trigger-happy men.

"Actually, Jesus is anything but weak." Haytham shifted his head away from the gun barrel and eyed the man standing beside him.

The second man, who had stood in the doorway of the apartment, stepped toward Haytham, who was seated in the center of the room. The man holding the gun waved him off with the pistol, then pointed it at the ceiling. "Then why didn't He get off the cross if He was so powerful? Answer that, Mr. Christian!" He leaned in and spat past Haytham's cheek.

The pastor turned to face the men in his living room. "He didn't *want* to get off the cross. That was the whole reason He came in the first place—my sins, *your* sins, had to be paid for."

"The way I plan to pay for my sins is to blow your head off!" The sweaty man brought the gun down, pointed it at Haytham's temple, and pulled the trigger.

Singing gave way to a moving foot-washing service. New Alawite believers brought out bowls of water and washed the feet of Sunni believers. Farid, Joseph, and more than a dozen others broke into tears. Sobbing continued as the Sunni Christians took their turn. One Alawite wailed in joyful grief and kissed the head of a Sunni man washing his feet. The ritual stopped, and the two men embraced, tears drenching each other's shoulders.

Farid overheard another Sunni sigh as he toweled the feet of an Alawite: "Please forgive me for how my people have treated your people. Jesus washed feet out of love and humility. I do this for you in the same spirit."

For two hours, worship enveloped Farid, Joseph, and Hanna. As the singing, prayer, and foot-washing ebbed, Majeed Husain, the brother of an Alawite sheikh, motioned the group to sit down on the floor. He remained standing as he spoke to the assembly.

"The Lord brought all of us together. For months I wondered why I was having the dreams. I could not shake them. I finally read the New Testament and was shocked to find in the book of Matthew that Jesus said, 'Follow Me.' In each of my dreams he had said that to *me*.

"When I received Jesus, my heart was filled with love, and I could no longer hate. One day Kamal invited me to visit over tea." He nodded at a man sitting on the floor to his right. "The invitation was a great risk.

"I was overcome with joy to find out I was not alone. Other people were meeting Jesus too. Many had dreams like mine.

"Think of it: Kamal, from a Sunni family, led me, from an Alawite family, to Jesus, who was from a Jewish family, so I could join the Christian family." Laughter rippled across the room. "What an amazing peace plan that is!"

Kamal stood up and stepped next to Majeed. Majeed nodded and sat down.

Kamal picked up the message. "For years Sunnis and Alawites lived side by side. Oh, we had our differences. But this war split our nation in half. I have seen more death in the last four years than in the other forty years of my life. But Jesus loves Syria." He looked down at the man who had just finished speaking. "Majeed, my brother, Matthew also says in chapter 4, 'News about Him spread all over Syria.'

"And this is why we are here. He has called us out. Out of the world, out of this war, out of our families to stand for Him in Syria!" Kamal paused and slowly scanned the audience. He looked every individual in the eye before he spoke again. "This will cost us our lives. We will die for this. The Jesus message is upside down compared to the ethnic and religious hatred that's destroying our country.

"But while the enemy comes to divide, we will conquer him *together*. Satan is rejoicing at all the death around us." Kamal smirked. "He thinks he has won, but soon Jesus will *crush* him. And Jesus will go on doing what only He can do. Only Jesus can bring together every tribe, language, people, and nation. Only Jesus can clean a heart controlled by hate."

After Kamal and Majeed concluded their messages, the gathering disbursed, one or two people at a time, silently ascending the stairs into the darkness above. It was nearly 3:00 a.m. when Hanna showed Farid and Joseph to an empty room upstairs where they could stay the night. Farid's heart filled with peace as he dropped off to sleep on the carpeted floor.

The cell phone startled Farid awake. He squinted at faint light seeping between the closed curtains. The sun was not fully up yet. He pressed the talk button and began the call he dreaded—news of that night's terrorist rampage in Latakia, his parents' hometown.

But he was relieved to hear his father's voice. He could make out his mother's crying in the background as Haytham Assad recounted the gut-wrenching encounter with two terrorists in the dark hours of that morning. One had promised to kill him and pulled the trigger of an unloaded gun next to his head.

In its door-to-door campaign to eliminate infidels, the al-Nusra Front, an al-Qaeda–spawned terrorist group, demanded conversion to Islam or a ransom for anyone who would not pray the Shahada.* If the non-Muslim could not—or would not—pay, a bullet to the head ended negotiations quickly. They had

---

* A Muslim creed that declares, "There is no god but Allah, and Muhammad is his messenger."

already left a grisly trail of non-converts before arriving in Farid's parents' neighborhood.

Haytham Assad explained few details to his son, but Farid knew his parents' situation was dire. Last night, he had wept for joy in the sweet worship service, but this morning as he hung up the phone, Farid sobbed in grief for his mom and dad.

Although Haytham had downplayed the circumstances, Farid knew his father would not compromise with the terrorists. Conversion was not a possibility. His dad would never sell out in any way. He had often spoken of dying for Jesus as if he sensed that was his destiny.

Still sitting on the floor where he had slept, Farid calmed himself, wiping tears from his cheeks, and made a decision. He would go to his parents and take them to a safe house. He would insist they go. Farid closed his eyes and prayed that he would get to them in time. Then he crawled across the room and tapped Hanna's shoulder. The sleeping man stirred.

"Hanna, we must go now."

Joseph stayed behind. He would find another way home. So only Farid and Hanna sped north from Damascus. The two men evaluated their chances of making it to Latakia. In the best of conditions, the treacherous journey would take three and a half hours, but Homs lay between Damascus and Latakia. Checkpoints through the city would almost certainly cause problems. And then there was the fighting. Farid spelled out for Hanna what he knew of the situation there.

"Homs is under siege right now, and our highway goes right through it. If we make it, there will probably be no way back once we make the turn to head west at Homs." Farid paused in thought. "I have a friend in the area who will know what's happening there. I'll call him to see how things are today."

Farid grabbed the phone from his pocket and scrolled through the contact list. He tapped his friend's number.

"Mosab! Yes. I'm all right. I'm on my way to Latakia. What can you tell me about the situation in Homs?" Hanna glanced repeatedly at Farid and watched the color drain from his face as he listened to the voice on the other end of the call. Farid gasped.

"No! That's *horrible*. How many? When?" Farid paused again, listening. "Yes, Mosab. We'll be careful."

Farid ended the call and sat staring at his phone. Hanna drove in silence for what seemed like an eternity. He looked intermittently at his friend, both wanting and fearing to know what Farid had just heard.

After several minutes, Farid, still plaintively eyeing the phone in his hand as if it might yet take back the words it had delivered, spoke softly. "Seven men were beheaded on the outskirts of Homs this morning. All young believers. Mosab said they were tortured first."

Farid jerked his head up and looked straight at Hanna. "Mosab says we should turn around." He examined his friend's face for a reaction, but Hanna just drove.

"You know I can't go back, right?"

Hanna cut his eyes toward Farid. "Of course you can't.

And neither can I!" He jammed the gas pedal and accelerated toward Homs.

Twenty minutes from Homs, the Hyundai raced through surprisingly light traffic. Farid and Hanna speculated that troops were needed more urgently somewhere else and had left checkpoints, completely unguarded. Nevertheless, they knew other dangers lay ahead.

"Farid, you pray while I drive. We're not far from the turnoff in Homs toward Latakia. We've been okay so far, but I have a bad feeling about what might be ahead."

Eyes open and studying the view for problems, Farid prayed quietly for guidance and protection. For several minutes the two men said nothing to each other as Hanna joined Farid in silent prayer.

The car looped onto Ring Road, where the highway bends west toward the coast. As the Elantra swung off the ramp onto a straight stretch, Farid abruptly pointed ahead. A group of a dozen or so armed men were running toward the highway from across a field several hundred yards to the right. Brake lights flashed on a handful of cars about a half mile ahead, as the crack of gunfire echoed across the open space. Knowing many of the armaments used by terrorist groups, Farid recognized British-made AS50 sniper rifles. The men in the field had stopped and opened fire on passing vehicles.

As Hanna and Farid sped toward the scene, three cars swerved simultaneously and glanced off of each other, their drivers unlucky targets of the random assault. A red Kia Rio spun off the right side of the road and flipped in a ditch. Another Kia slid sideways down the left lane, and the third car, a Hyundai, rocketed to the left, taking a nearby motorcycle with it into the median.

Quickly recognizing that stopping meant certain death, Hanna accelerated into the chaos. Two more cars just ahead took fire and swerved off the road, leaving an opening in the traffic. Farid dropped to the floor of the Elantra as Hanna straddled the two lanes and surged through the space, leaving the clatter of rifle fire behind. Hanna and Farid looked at each other, wide-eyed.

Ninety minutes later, Farid and Hanna tiptoed up the stairway to Farid's parents' apartment. At the door, Farid raised his hand, signaling Hanna to wait, and pressed his left ear against the wooden surface. Hearing nothing inside, he gently twisted the doorknob. It was unlocked!

"Mom? Dad?" Farid stepped inside, scanning the apartment. Haytham and Suhad Assad sat at the kitchen table. They looked up from their tea as Farid entered, and smiled. For several seconds, the younger man stood gazing at his parents, alive and well.

"The two men I told you about on the phone," Haytham continued the story he couldn't bring himself to finish on the phone five hours earlier, "promised to be back tomorrow morning to witness my conversion or accept the ransom money to save my life." His smile drooped. "They want ten thousand dollars. Ha! They know I don't have that much money. I told them I'm a pastor!"

Their son blinked, nodded, stepped into the kitchen, and hugged his parents.

Farid made a phone call to confirm the plans for protecting his father and mother, and by dinnertime, Haytham and Suhad were sitting together on a couch in the living room of an apartment an hour's drive south along the Mediterranean coast. Halfway to the safe house, Farid's father had insisted on stopping to visit a Muslim family.

"Farid, I know you think I was foolish to go to their house, but they called me just yesterday. The father has had eight Jesus dreams this month. He had questions."

Farid shook his head and sighed. "Dad, I wouldn't expect you to make your escape in any other way! I know you never miss an opportunity to visit with someone about Jesus—ever."

The community surrounding the apartment had so far been spared the systematic purges happening in larger cities. Hanna, Farid, and Farid's parents would spend a peaceful night together here. The following day, Hanna and Farid would return to Damascus to prepare for the next night's meeting.

In the morning, all agreed that Haytham and Suhad would stay at the safe house as long as necessary. Latakia was simply too dangerous to go back to right away, and Damascus was unstable enough that Farid could not be sure his parents would be any safer there with him. So in the afternoon, Farid and Hanna headed back to Damascus, leaving Haytham and Suhad protected for now.

The return to Damascus was remarkably uneventful. By swinging east around the top of the city before driving into town, they avoided the worst of the trouble spots. Hanna's neighborhood was blessedly calm when they arrived, and the two men breathed a prayer of thanks together, even if the respite was only temporary.

That night, ten leaders from among the local believers arrived at a non-descript basement, silently and on schedule at 2:00 a.m. The group of men exchanged wordless greetings and crowded into the meeting room. Once everyone was seated, Farid stood and addressed them in a voice slightly above a whisper.

"If we don't leave with our families soon, I'm not sure we will ever get out alive. Two nights ago, my father in Latakia was threatened with a gun to his head, and Hanna and I barely made it through Homs alive. It seems that utter chaos is normal for Syria now." Farid paused, eyeing his fellow believers. "I have to wonder if this is really the place to raise our children. We must pray for God's direction. I call for a week of fasting.

"In Scripture, King Hezekiah faced a deadly situation in Jerusalem similar to ours. The Assyrian king Sennacherib publicly threatened to destroy Jerusalem—a threat he was fully capable of carrying out. On his own, Hezekiah could not stand against Sennacherib's death machine. The Assyrian had already left a path of destruction through what is now our country and Lebanon as well, on his way to Israel."

Farid raised his right hand and pointed to the ceiling. "But Hezekiah was so dependent on the Lord that he resisted the urge to do anything. He took the threatening letter from the Assyrian king and laid it open before the Lord on the temple steps.

"Hezekiah sought the Lord. He prayed. And he waited—but not for long." Farid smiled. "God answered the next day. He sent an angel, who annihilated the Assyrian army on the outskirts of Jerusalem."

Farid paused again and folded his hands in front of his chest before continuing. "This is a time like that. Only God has the answer. Starting tonight, for the next seven days, let's each lay out this question before the Lord. Do we stay in Syria or go? For one week, let us cease all activities except the greatest one of all—prayer.

"After that, if God calls you and your family to leave, begin the journey as fast as you can. If He calls you to stay, meet back here one week from tonight at this same time."

Farid opened his hands and spread them toward the group. "His plan for you may be different from His plan for me. That is okay, and there is no pressure to decide one way or the other. None of us are trying to be heroes. We want God's will for us and for our families. Whether we stay *or* go, we take Jesus' message of love and forgiveness with us." A dozen men nodded in concert.

Farid closed his eyes and raised his hands above his head. "Now, let's pray and be dismissed."

Seven days later, chaos still reigned in the streets of

Damascus. Gun battles consumed a dozen square blocks along Farid's first route to the follow-up meeting, and damaged roads slowed progress on his alternate route. He arrived thirty minutes late, wondering if he would walk into an empty room. Although he had been serious when he said no one should feel pressured to stay, he hoped at least one or two others would have come to the same conclusion he had. He would face martyrdom alone if it came to that, but having fellowship with a few other believers in the meantime would be an encouragement.

Farid descended the steps from the sidewalk and paused at the door. He grasped the doorknob and turned it slowly. Dim light appeared as the door swung open. Farid's jaw dropped. Twenty-five men, seated on the floor, looked up at him. The ten leaders from last week's meeting had returned—along with fifteen new disciples.

Each of the leaders told his story of how God had led him to stay, and a handful of newcomers shared testimonies. The sober joy of their decisions to remain in Syria brought them to a point of business few believers ever have to discuss. The men agreed to pool their funds and buy a plot of land, preparing for what would certainly come. It would be the graveyard in which they would bury each other.

## A MESSAGE FROM FARID

So many brothers and sisters have been killed already that it seems our little group has the only empty graveyard in Syria. As of this writing, none of us have died yet. We rejoice by greeting one another with the words, "The graveyard is still empty!" We all know it will not *stay* empty, but meanwhile, we're grateful.

Satan rampages through Syria, the lion fighting to annihilate the church. Torture and killing continues every day, and each month, we hear of new terrorist groups forming. All seem intent on outdoing one another in committing unspeakable evils.

I think what followers of Christ in Syria fear most are the crucifixions. It's a horrifying prospect. Death on a cross is gruesome, and on top of that, crowds mock and torture the believers leading up to actually nailing them onto crosses.

Some who face this are new in the faith, and I don't blame them for being frightened, but it would be an honor to die for Jesus in this way. Just think: the Lamb of God went to the cross in Jerusalem only two hundred miles from Damascus. Now, two thousand years later, the prospect hangs over our heads as a real possibility, just like it did for Jesus and His followers in the first century.

But regardless of which of us end up literally crucified for Christ, the question is: Have we not died already? Paul—who was converted right here in Syria—proclaimed, "I am crucified with Christ."

I consider Syrian believers fortunate to have a tangible reminder of this fact. Why? Because I used to think I lived a life of sacrifice, but that changed when the war broke out. Although Syria has so few believers that there was danger before, I did not really know what it means to sacrifice. *What I thought was sacrifice was actually just inconvenience.*

Once we bought the graveyard, we gave up our right to live as we pleased. We consigned ourselves to a violent death—whether a sudden bullet in the brain, beheading, or a torturous crucifixion. Our lives rest in God's hands.

There is remarkable freedom in having no expectations, no plans for tomorrow. The question I and many others start every day with is this: "Jesus, what do You have planned for me and my family?" Only today matters. Only how I live for Jesus counts. Everything else is superficial. When I hand over my life to my Lord, knowing each day may be my last one on this earth, I am more at peace than ever before.

One of my heroes from the past is Jerome, who translated the Bible into Latin, the common language of the people in the fourth century AD. He was so driven to make each day count for Christ in order to complete the task God gave him that he lived with an unusual reminder of how precious each day is. He chained a skull to his ankle to help him remember he was always just one breath away from the end of his life. Jerome used to say, "Another hour has passed for which I must give an account to Christ."

*Is your life about Jesus and nothing else?* When you may die at any moment, it has to be that way, but we're all called to live only for Him, no matter what.

Although Paul once sacrificed Christians, he met Jesus, gave up all his "rights," and made himself a living sacrifice. Once you live like this, you grasp the most profound fulfillment possible in life.

Pray for us in Syria, but please do not feel bad for us. We have never been more free. And even though we're willing to die, our graveyard is still empty.

# CHAPTER THREE

# SYRIAN REFUGEE, BUT NOT FORGOTTEN

THESE ARE THE names of Ishmael's sons; their names according to the family records are: Nebaioth, Ishmael's firstborn, then Kedar, Adbeel, Mibsam, Mishma, Dumah, Massa, Hadad, Tema, Jetur, Naphish, and Kedemah.*

To Rafiq, *Hadad*, the eighth name in the ancient record of his family lineage, was the sweetest. Pride blended with a touch of humor as he often pointed out to associates and friends that his family took up residence in Damascus only two generations after Abraham pitched his tent in Hebron. The Hadads had been a prominent fixture in this Syrian community for centuries, arguably for several millennia.

Yet Rafiq Hadad's vast legacy and the connections he had

---

*Gen. 25:13–15 HCSB; emphasis added.

amassed through the seven thriving businesses he personally built in Damascus seemed unable to help him now—and his wife was worried.

"Mother, where's father?" Hania Hadad's head appeared in the mirror of her mother's bathroom.

"I expect him home any minute, *habibti.*"* Dori Hadad's eyes glanced at the image of the fifteen-year-old girl standing behind her in the doorway, then back to her own face.

The mother raised her index fingers to her forehead, smoothed the eyebrows, and studied her makeup to be sure it was just right, as she did every night before Rafiq arrived home. Whatever he might notice about other women, she was determined not to give him reason to ignore her. Flawless olive skin, precisely enhanced with a trace of color, offset captivating green eyes. Dori was satisfied and hoped Rafiq would be too—at least for the evening.

She stared at her reflection for several seconds more, then sighed. Her eyes drooped to the cell phone resting on the counter by her left hand. Rafiq had promised to be home at six o'clock sharp. And he had meant his own, disciplined *sharp* time, not standard "Arabic time." The Damascus power couple kept close tabs on each other as the now four-year-long Syrian war grew more dangerous each day.

A viable defense against peacetime thieves, their gated community offered little more than a distraction to militant Sunnis in their quest to eradicate Alawite government officials and anyone who appeared friendly toward them. Yet the Hadad home—

*My beloved.

large enough to house twenty average Syrian families—provided one *helpful* distraction to the terrorists, one that Dori hoped was in her husband's favor again tonight. It advertised the family's considerable wealth, and so far, Rafiq's pursuers had been satisfied with his offers to buy weapons for their cause and had not insisted on his bodily participation in the fighting. Over the last several years, Rafiq had purchased hundreds of weapons and countless rounds of ammunition for the Free Syrian Army.

*A late business meeting?* Dori wondered. But she could not muster much hope to believe that business as usual had detained her husband tonight. Both feared the day would come when the FSA would demand more than Rafiq's cash. No man could prove his ultimate dedication to the cause without personal service in the campaign to oust Bashar Assad. For everyone, the time always came when service—and likely death later—had to be chosen over avoidance, and certain death immediately.

Whether in business or war, Rafiq Hadad was a pragmatist. To maintain the expedient image of a practicing Sunni Muslim, Rafiq appeared at least weekly at Jumu'ah. Friday prayers were mandatory, and the Umayyad Mosque—the "Great Mosque of Damascus"—offered the perfect place for a prominent businessman to make an obvious appearance. But Jumu'ah was nothing more than another appointment on Rafiq's overflowing calendar, an appointment necessary to keep his customers happy. Any heartfelt religious conviction in the soul of this Hadad family member had left him long ago. Killings in the name of Allah squelched all connection he may have once felt for Islam.

Rafiq's fervent-looking practice masked the dangerous

preferences he harbored for the sake of his business. The Syrian economy would be far better off if President Bashar al-Assad and the Alawites managed to stay in power. The Assad family knew how to keep Islamic fanatics in check.

Hafez al-Assad, Bashar's father, had ruled Syria with an intricate secret police system that infiltrated every stratum of society. To maintain his grip, the previous Assad had once leveled the city of Hama and killed thousands of Sunnis who rebelled against him. The massacre had taken only a few days and delivered the wanted effect. Syria became an Arabic version of an Iron Curtain nation. No one dared throw stones at its ruthless leader.

Bashar al-Assad had learned the lessons of power well from his father, yet now Rafiq feared the end was near for the stabilizer of the one thing Hadad held dear: the means to make money, and lots of it. Sunni fundamentalists—driven by their ridiculous convictions instead of the desire for tangible rewards in this life—believed they were well on their way to overthrowing Assad. Three-fourths of Syria now claimed to be Sunni. Bashar would not be able to hold back the tide, but Rafiq wanted nothing to do with this mindless religious uprising.

Dori's love for the finer things in life made her the ideal mate for a Hadad male. Trips to Europe, long weekends in Dubai, an overnight stay at Lebanon's finest hotel so she could eat at her favorite restaurant, all perfectly suited her self-image. Like her husband, she struggled to portray an appropriate Muslim lifestyle. And like many of her friends, she simply maintained two separate lives—the one matching expectations of fellow Syrians, and the other fulfilling her own whims and pleasures when she was out of the country.

In Syria, her children learned the Quran and acted the part of faithful Muslims. By every appearance, Hania and her year-younger brother, Saeeb, lived in a devoted Islamic family under the direction of a strong Islamic mother. But beyond children, love of money, and the facade of Islam, Dori and Rafiq shared nothing worthwhile.

Being at home was as much "business" to Rafiq as managing his real estate holdings or one of his jewelry stores. Daily, he extended necessary pleasantries, but beneath the surface charm Rafiq controlled everything ruthlessly. His indifference toward Dori's heart needs drove her to a refuge of which she was not proud but which she was not willing to relinquish either. The intimacy she desired from her husband she found instead in the arms of a neighbor. The female friend endured a lifeless marriage similar to Dori's and welcomed the warmth the two women shared. Any shame they might have felt dissolved in their mutual need, and besides, their situation—and its solution—was not uncommon among the women they knew.

Still, Rafiq was the father of Dori's children, and despite their meaningless relationship, she enjoyed the security of his presence at home. Even if business had become Rafiq's mistress—and there were rumors of others as well—Dori would have taken back every tear she had cried over Rafiq's coldness just to hear him crack a joke as he stepped into the house. But tonight only silence greeted her from the front door.

*Why didn't we just go on to Lebanon yesterday like we had planned?*

Although Rafiq had agreed with his wife as recently as that morning that his days of freedom were numbered and they would have to leave soon, he always had one more deal to do before he could go. Today may have been one too many.

He insisted that business drew him back, but Dori suspected it was more than just another twenty-four hours' worth of financial success that called to him. The stunning-from-head-to-toe young sales associate at Hadad Jewelers seemed to Dori a little too friendly toward her husband. *And why are there new female employees every few weeks?*

A familiar ring tone from Dori's cell phone jolted her out of the thoughts. She picked up the device from the bathroom counter.

"Rafiq?"

"No, Dori. This is Hassan." Dori's forehead wrinkled at the sound of her brother-in-law's voice. A call from him was unexpected. "It seems my brother has been taken. He was led out of his office with hands tied behind his back."

Dori gasped. "When?"

"Just now. Dori, you must go! You must go *now*—for Hania and Saeeb's sake. None of you are safe in Damascus anymore. I think you should head to Jordan."

"Are you sure?" Dori knew the implications of Hassan's suggestion.

"I know what you'll be leaving behind if you go, Dori, but if you stay, it will be much worse. These scum will almost certainly take Hania for *use* by those filthy terrorists. And Saeeb will become front-lines fodder to fight for the FSA."

Hassan paused to let Dori feel the impact of his warning. Then he continued, softly but in a tone that disallowed any argument. "It will take about four days to get across the border. You cannot trust anyone to help you, but you must get to Jordan. And, Dori"—the man on the phone paused again—"you must go *tonight*."

Dori closed her eyes and pressed her left hand to her temple. "But, Hassan, can't we leave in the morning? We could be gone by sunrise."

"No, Dori. You are in serious, *immediate* danger. These people know Rafiq keeps money hidden at the house. They may be headed your way right now. Take some cash for yourself, and lock the rest of it in the safe. As soon as possible, I will come get it and keep it for you and my brother." Hassan hesitated. "If he is still alive."

Also enough of a pragmatist to accept the desperation of her circumstances, Dori ignored the emotion that threatened to erupt at the thought her husband might be dead and responded soberly. "How much do you think I should take with me?"

"Not much. Maybe a hundred pounds. The fact is, Dori, you'll probably be robbed as soon as you get to the Zaatari refugee camp in Jordan. Meanwhile, money may help keep you safe. I hope you can be back in a few weeks, and I hope you and Rafiq will be together again. I really do."

Hassan's sister-in-law squelched a sniffle.

"Dori, *go*."

The woman in the mirror nodded as her phone went silent.

Ten minutes later, Hania finally stopped crying, but Saeeb took the news about his father and the family's imminent departure stoically. Using his mother as a witness, he swore to Allah that he would one day avenge whatever was now happening to his father. He vowed to summon the powerful Hadad family to join his fight of retribution.

The three Hadads piled selected necessities on the floor in Dori's bedroom. The mother edited the choices and stuffed the final assortment into a single black gym bag. Since she knew calling a taxi would be dangerous—cab drivers were well connected and known to be the best informants around—she looked each of her children in the eye and said simply, "Let's go."

The threesome slipped out the back door and walked softly across the yard and around the house. Dori raised her hand, and the group paused behind the side yard gate. Saeeb stepped close to his mother. He joined her in scanning the front yard and street along the far edge of the Hadad property. Dori and her son nodded at each other, and the two of them plus Hania headed across the open space.

Dori glanced back for a last look at her prestigious Mezzah neighborhood home. She hoped her memories of life here would not become as dim as the moonlight on her residential prize. Saeeb reached for his mother's hand, took the gym bag, and the three refugees scurried into the shadowy street.

An hour into their trek, Dori, Saeeb, and Hania walked undisturbed through side streets just off Fayez Mansour, knowing that travel along the main road would likely bring unwanted encounters. Dori said nothing to her children about the foreboding sign she could not ignore as they had walked southwest toward the edge of Damascus. Each of the embassies they passed—Greece, Finland, Switzerland, even Malaysia—was *empty. When did everyone leave?* she wondered.

They turned south, and on the outskirts of the city, Dori reluctantly chose the main highway for their sixty-five-mile dash to safety. She was not sure how else she would find the way to Jordan. To lighten the mood, Dori turned their hike into an educational opportunity for the children.

"Saeeb. Hania." Brother and sister glanced up at their mother as they walked. "This is the King's Highway we're on. People in our family centuries ago may well have journeyed along here, just like we're doing. It has been here since the time of the prophet Abraham. His son—our father—Ishmael walked this road himself." Dori touched her son's shoulder. "Saeeb, do you remember what the name 'Ishmael' means?"

Saeeb huffed and kicked a piece of gravel, swirling dust into the air. "'Allah hears.' You know I know that, Mother."

Dori nodded. "You know the facts, Saeeb. Now we will all learn what it *means*. We're in serious trouble, but Allah will hear our cries for help, just like he did with Ishmael."

For the first time since they had left home, Hania spoke. "It looks like we're not the only ones in need of help from Allah, Mother." She pointed ahead.

Arriving at the four-thousand-year-old highway, Dori and the two children had joined a sparse but steady stream of people leaving Damascus on foot. Dori estimated that thirty or forty others hiked the half-mile-long stretch of road in front of them. The dim light of the moon would not reveal how many more may range beyond that. Many, she assumed.

At what should have been breakfast time, the travelers approached a large intersection south of Damascus.

"Mother, what are those people clapping and shouting about?" Hania stopped beside Dori, who was studying the scene thirty yards ahead.

Several hundred agitated people—mostly men—blocked the crossroads. Chanting arose from the din, harsh voices repeating, "There is no god but Allah, and Muhammad is his messenger!"

Before Dori could answer Hania's question, a gap opened in the crowd. The Hadads were too close to comfortably bear what they saw. From ropes thrown over a utility wire swung two naked corpses—one male and one female—feet just off the ground. Blood dribbled from what was left of their faces, and internal organs dangled from gaping chest cavities. The dead couple had been cruelly tortured before the hanging.

Hania grasped the sides of her face and vomited the little that remained in her stomach. Dori closed her eyes and chewed her upper lip while Saeeb stared coldly at the dead bodies. Evidently hoping for media coverage, two men in the crowd paraded a large sign proclaiming their goal:

*Infidels!*
*We slay all converts and anyone who disgraces Islam.*
*Al-Nusra\* is the voice of Islam.*
*We will wash the streets of Damascus in Christian blood!*
*While Christians celebrate Easter this week around the*
*world, Syrians will show what fate awaits them in the*
*coming global jihad.*

After several seconds, Saeeb pressed his hands together, touched them to his chin, and snarled. "They got what they deserved."

Dori's eyes popped open and riveted on her son's face. "Saeeb! What do you mean?"

Saeeb slowly turned toward his mother and spoke without emotion. "A Muslim converting to Christianity. Someone must have paid them to do it. I wish the same would happen to everyone who calls himself 'Christian.'" He looked back at the raucous mob. "Allah has repaid these people for their deed."

Dori eyed the crowd, then looked again at her son, and spoke quietly, shaking her head. "I'm not sure it was Allah that did this, Saeeb. Christians and Muslims have lived in peace here for centuries. It's this war that has made them hate the Christians."

Saeeb's eyes questioned his mother's assertion.

"This is *evil*, Saeeb! Terrorists did this in the name of religion. You don't see Christians hanging Muslims in the streets, do you?"

Saeeb would not relinquish. "No, Mother, you don't. They know that we would slaughter *all* the Christians if that ever

---

\* A Syrian branch of al-Qaeda.

happened. They can't beat us." Saeeb paused, staring at Dori. Then he continued caustically, "But why defend them, Mother? They're Jew-lovers, too, which makes them almost as low as those sickening Jews in Palestine."

Saeeb turned, took three steps toward the chaos, dropped the gym bag, and joined the clapping. Dori jumped after him and grabbed his hands.

"Saeeb! No!"

The boy wrenched his hands from his mother's and turned to face her. "What? Mother, are you a convert or something? You're starting to sound like a Christian yourself!"

Dori resisted the urge to slap her son's face. "My dear, perhaps a bit too arrogant, Saeeb," Dori controlled her tone, "I'm a Muslim, and nothing can change that. But not all of us think like this." She waved her hand at the monstrosity. "Murder is murder, no matter what label *any* religion puts on it." She stopped abruptly. Her left hand jerked to her mouth, and she gasped. Dori *recognized* the victims.

Her eyes flashed at her son, and she screamed, "Saeeb, do you not know who these people are? They are the Husseins! You used to play with their son Mohammad growing up."

The boy stared, passionless, at his mother.

She lowered her voice and continued in disgust. "No, Saeeb, they did not convert for money. They had plenty of it—even more than we do. They had to have other reasons." She shook her head and looked at the ground. "Perhaps reasons we can't understand."

Saeeb sneered, raised his hands toward the bloody scene,

and clapped once, loudly. With all the disdain he could muster, the young man cut his eyes sideways and glared at his mother.

Dori straightened, squinting defiantly at the murderous throng. She snatched their belongings from the ground at Saeeb's feet, turned her back on her son, and walked over to Hania. Dori wrapped an arm around the girl's shoulder. "Are you all right, Hania?"

The girl nodded.

Her mother pointed toward the crowd. "This is horrible! We have to get away."

She pulled Hania toward the edge of the road, directing her around the violence. Saeeb watched them, nodded once more at the dead bodies, then followed his mother and sister.

Four days later, Dori, Hania, and Saeeb trudged into a holding facility at Quneitra, two miles shy of Jordan. Syria had one last, misery-inducing stop for everyone crossing the border. Dori estimated that nearly five hundred people stood within this refugee "camp"—a ten-foot-high fence encircling a bare patch of sand no more than one hundred feet in diameter. Once inside, Dori discovered the holding tank offered neither food nor toilets.

"This is inhumane!" Dori yelled at a guard standing just outside the wire enclosure.

Wordless, his face responded: "I couldn't care less about you or your family."

*No wonder refugees are always considered the world's forgotten people*. Dori would save tears over their situation for later. For now, she would have to figure a way to save her children.

Three minutes after midnight on the second night of their stay, Dori knelt at the fence. With Hania and Saeeb screening her movement, she scooped sand from under the wire. In minutes, she had carved a hole large enough for her slender form to slip beneath the fence. Twenty-four hours into their stay, the three Hadads had eaten nothing, and Dori's desperate plan to find food had taken shape in her mind. Sprinting for the highway, her black *hijab* became the perfect nighttime camouflage. No one saw her.

At the highway, she flagged down a truck. The driver pulled off the road and opened the door. Yes, he would help. He had food, but he wanted a sample of what was hidden beneath her clothing first. Although fearful of being taken by force, Dori refused. The man spit on the ground beside the lone woman and drove off.

The roadside drama repeated itself three more times, but the fourth driver responded to her refusal as Dori had feared each one might. His powerful right arm grabbed her around the head, pulled her into the cab, and onto the seat beside him. But he had not counted on Dori to resist. Her free right hand smashed the man's nose. He shouted in pain and released his grip on Dori's head. She fell from the seat, rolled several feet from the large vehicle, and lay facedown in the sand. She heard the door slam as the truck accelerated onto the highway.

Scrambling to her feet, Dori winced at the blast of a horn.

She peered over her shoulder as a semi braked to a halt at the spot the other truck had just left. The door swung open, and a man jumped to the ground. He raised his arms toward Dori.

"I saw what happened! I won't hurt you! I want to help."

Dori sized up the new stranger and believed him. "I need food."

"I have bread. Do you need water, too?"

"Yes. For me and for my children."

The man nodded and turned to the truck. He extracted several bags from a compartment under the cab.

"Here. This is yours." He approached Dori and handed her bags containing several bottles of water and four uncut loaves of bread. As she took the provisions, her helper looked at her kindly. "Begging along the highway could get you killed—or at the very least kidnapped and sold on the black market. Whatever is wrong, I hope you'll be careful."

Dori stiffened. "My children are hungry, and my husband is missing. It was the only thing left to do."

"I understand." The man paused and then bowed slightly in Dori's direction. "My name is Osama. It's an honor to help you. I pray this tides you over until you are safe in Jordan. I assume that's where you're going."

The man had read the situation well. "I'm Dori, and yes, I'm going to Jordan." Dori looked at the ground and shook her head. "I can never thank you enough."

The stranger's next words startled the grateful woman: "The Lord Jesus bless you, Dori. Look to *Him*. He will be your shelter."

Dori cocked her head and looked at the man's face for the first time. The two eyed each other for several seconds before Dori said, "Thank you." It was all she could think of to say. Why a Muslim man would suggest "the Lord Jesus bless you" was a mystery. She wasn't sure what the words meant, but a sensation of peace rippled through her heart when she heard them.

Hania and Saeeb lay on the ground by the hole under the fence. Neither had slept since their mother had left three hours earlier, and both caught sight of the dark form as soon as Dori scurried into the open space between the fence wire and the road.

At the fence, Dori beckoned the two children to crawl under and join her. The three escapees ran hard away from the camp and darted across the road. Thirty minutes later, they stopped to eat at the base of a cliff on the Jordan side of a mountain pass. Then, stomachs satisfied, they tucked themselves behind a row of boulders to sleep.

The threesome awoke at sunrise and strolled into Jordan, unnoticed. The sun warmed them as they angled across the sand in the direction of Zaatari.

An hour's walk put them within sight of the camp when a noise startled Dori. It was her cell phone. She had forgotten she had it with her and could hardly believe the battery wasn't dead. Dori pulled the phone from under her hijab, recognized the number, and touched the screen to answer the call.

"Hassan?"

"Yes, Dori. Where are you?"

Dori ignored the question. "Any word on my husband?"

"No, Dori. I'm sorry to say I've heard nothing yet about Rafiq. But I haven't heard about any new killings, either, so I think he's probably alive. I call for another reason, though. It's important I know exactly where you are."

"We're in Jordan, just inside the border. Why, Hassan?"

"I have new information about Zaatari. Whatever you do, Dori, stay away from the refugee camp! I mentioned to a friend that I knew someone who was going there—I didn't give him your name—and what he said worried me."

Dori pressed the phone hard against her ear.

"Apparently, the camp has been infiltrated by terrorists, and the situation is brutal. They will not protect you there. In fact, the men holding the camp will probably try to rape you.

"My friend even said families in the camp are so desperate, they're selling teenage daughters for as little as fifty dollars. One family he knows of agreed because they were told the girl would be returned to them in two weeks. But he's sure they'll never see her again. These are sex-slave buyers. The traffickers scope out the camp for girls like that—and Hania. Virgins bring a higher price."

Dori took a deep breath, peered ahead at the sea of white tents inside the camp, then stared into the sky, wondering what to do.

Hassan continued. "And Saeeb. He will be forced to join one of the terrorist groups. They won't give him a choice."

Dori shook her head. "So, Hassan, what do we do? I can see the camp from here. We're that close."

"Then I'm glad I caught you. Sidestep the camp and head south, all the way to Amman. I don't know why I didn't think of it before. There are thousands of undocumented refugees in the capital. You can fill out the necessary paperwork later, and meanwhile, you'll be much safer there."

"But where will we stay?"

"I've heard there are old apartments filled with Syrian refugees. You have enough money to pay for one. I'm guessing you would do best to head for the center of the city, close to the Roman amphitheater. I also know a few people in Amman who might be able to help you find a place to stay. I'll call them."

"You must be new here."

The two-day walk to Amman had given Hassan's friends time to find an apartment for Dori, Saeeb, and Hania. Her brother-in-law's contacts were secretive but efficient, and the three new refugees had a place to live, however Spartan. But the woman standing in the doorway of their apartment puzzled Dori.

"I don't remember seeing you, and I'm here every day." The stranger continued her awkward self-introduction. "We help with food and whatever we can to make this place livable."

"Are you with the United Nations?" Dori hoped for reason to trust this person.

"We're not with anyone, actually. The refugees call us 'the Bible people.'" She smiled bashfully. "We like that name."

Dori scanned the woman's face. Then her eyes settled on the package in the visitor's arms.

"My name is Samar. About the only affiliation I have is that I'm a follower." She held the bundle toward Dori. "Here's some food for you and your children. It will get you started— chickpeas, olive oil, beans, pita bread, and spices. Oh, and some Lipton Tea as well."

Dori reached silently for the parcel.

"I'm afraid the portable stove doesn't work too great, but it will warm some tea water. I'll be back later this week." Samar's lips stretched into a warm smile. "Welcome to Amman."

Dori did not smile in return. She could not understand why this was happening but managed a gracious response nonetheless. "Thank you, Samar. This means so much to have someone just . . ." She glanced at the package in her hands and back at Samar. "I mean . . . Do you want any money for this bag of groceries?"

"Of course not." Samar shook her head. "We're just happy to have you in Jordan. All of us pray that God will meet your every need here." She touched Dori's hand. "He loves you."

Dori shifted the package to her right arm. Two fingers and the thumb of her left hand gently grasped Samar's outstretched hand. "You said you are a follower. Of whom? Do you mean you work for King Abdullah?"

"No. I don't work for King Abdullah. He's a very good man, though, and we Jordanians love him just like we loved his father, King Hussein." She patted Dori's hand. "But I work for another King." She pulled back her hand and turned to leave.

"By the way, I'm Dori."

Samar smiled again. "Good night, Dori." She looked past

the refugee woman to Saeeb and Hania, who had been listening, wide-eyed, from behind their mother. "You children take good care of your mom."

The warm encounter with Samar that evening gave way to a cold and frightening night. Lying uncovered on the bare concrete floor kept sleep away from the weary new residents, but all would have preferred even bad dreams about what they'd been through so far to the nightmare of sounds around them.

Shrieks of pain reverberated in the alley outside their apartment. Two doors down something terrible was happening.

*Who is being beaten now—and why?* Dori wondered. She lay still and disciplined her breathing to sound relaxed, hoping her children would take comfort in thinking their mother was asleep and unworried.

*This is more than just another husband beating his wife.* She felt the evil.

The screams continued but grew weaker as the night deepened. After several hours, exhaustion had its way with the three Hadads, and all slipped into a welcome sleep. They would remember their first night in Jordan.

Hania dipped pita bread thoughtfully into the *zatar** Dori had made from spices supplied by Samar. The girl had not spoken

---

* Mixed herbs and spices.

in the thirty minutes since she had woken up, several hours after sunrise. While such a long silence was unusual for Hania in the morning, Dori assumed her daughter was feeling the aftershock of what they had heard during the night. The alleyway was mercifully quiet this morning.

Hania's ceramic bowl clinked as the girl set it on the floor and looked at Dori. "Mother, I had a dream that lasted almost all night." She paused, evaluating what to say next. "A man in a white robe told me that we are safe now, and He would take care of us." She paused again, glanced at her bowl of zatar, and then back at Dori. "He said His name was Jesus."

Dori slowly dipped bread in olive oil and then into the zatar. "What else did He say, Hania?"

Hania was relieved at her mother's inviting response. "It was something very strange. He told me that He loves me. And, Mother, somehow I know that He does! I could see it in His eyes. And it wasn't just for the dream."

Dori stiffened as a shiver sputtered up her backbone.

"Sweetheart! I had the same dream!"

Hania's eyes darted from her mother to Saeeb, who sat, knees nearly touching his sister's, and simply stared at his mother.

"Allah must be smiling on us!" Dori folded her hands together and brought them to her lips. "He sent one of his prophets to greet us."

She looked at each of her children in turn. "We will go to the Grand Husseini Mosque today for prayer. The Jordanians also have clothes and other things we may be able to use. It's another walk, but it won't seem long after our trek from Damascus."

Three hours later, a crestfallen Dori plodded with her children past the Roman Theatre a half mile south of the Grand Husseini Mosque and headed for their apartment. Not only had he offered no help; the imam had accused them of thievery. "Like all Syrians, you steal like bandits!" he had screamed in their faces. The mosque wanted nothing to do with Syrian refugees.

Saeeb still held a cloth to a two-inch slice where his right cheek met a rock on the ground. Unfeeling crowds had shoved him off balance. All three were lucky not to have been trampled, and Dori was thankful the injury to Saeeb's face was not deep; merely painful. All Saeeb had wanted was a Nike sweatshirt he found in a pile of clothing he thought was meant for the taking.

As they headed south from an intersection near the ancient amphitheater, Dori's heart leapt at the sound of a familiar voice.

"Dori!"

She isolated the direction of the shout and focused on a woman waving at her from the sidewalk a dozen feet ahead.

"Dori! I'm so glad to see you!" In several quick steps, the woman closed the distance between her and Dori. "Remember me? I'm Samar."

"Remember you? How could I forget your kindness?!" Dori suppressed an impulse to embrace the woman. She wasn't sure what this new friend would make of something so bold as a hug in public.

"I'm on my way to the church." Samar reached for Dori's hand. "Would you like to come with me? They have clothes you might be able to use."

Dori recoiled involuntarily. "Thank you, Samar, but we were just at the mosque, and that turned out very badly. They want nothing to do with us there."

"Oh, Dori. Then you *must* come with me. You can pick out whatever you need and leave whenever you want to."

"But"—Dori was instantly puzzled again by Samar—"you said you're going to a *church*. Muslims aren't allowed there, are they?"

"Of course they are! Anyone is welcome."

Still, Dori hesitated. "We need clothes, but we hate to fight the crowds." She pointed to Saeeb's face.

"Oh, Dori. I'm sorry about your son, but don't worry. Everyone gets served. In fact, a lot of people like to stay and visit. You probably could use a few new friends. And the church has lots of food." Samar smiled coyly. "I'll bet you can smell the hummus already."

Smell the hummus they did—and consumed large amounts of it. The church provided the best meal the Hadads had had since leaving Syria. Giant boxes of clothes lined the walls of a large meeting room where nearly two hundred people picked leisurely through the assortment. The bounty generated camaraderie among shoppers as they compared their finds.

Samar had also been right about new friends and staying to visit. After three hours, Dori and the children were still having fun socializing at the church. Dori even mentioned the Jesus dreams to Samar.

Arms loaded with bags of clothes, Saeeb led the walk back to the Hadad apartment. Neither he nor Hania had said a word since leaving the church. Finally, with only three blocks left, Hania blurted out what had been on her mind.

"I don't care if we ever go back to that mosque!" Several passersby noticed the comment and eyed the girl sternly.

Saeeb stopped and turned abruptly to look at his sister. His quick movement startled Hania. "Me neither!"

Relieved that her comment had not angered her brother, she continued. "Why were those Bible people so nice to us? I mean, what do they get out of this anyway?"

Before either Dori or Saeeb could respond, a siren screeched past. An ambulance sped around the corner ahead of them and into their neighborhood. They heard the whine of the emergency vehicle die away just out of sight.

The three Hadads quickened their pace. Rounding the corner, they saw the ambulance, red lights still flashing. Another ambulance was already at the scene, where a dozen onlookers watched a team of four paramedics load two sheet-covered bodies onto gurneys. Dori recognized among the bystanders an acquaintance from an apartment a few doors down from theirs and walked over to her.

"Aisha, what happened?" Dori motioned toward the dismal scene. "How did they die?"

"They were killed." The woman shook her head. "They did the worst thing possible. They converted, Dori! How could they become Christians? The imam tried to beat sense into them, but he finally concluded they were insane. No one in his or her right mind would do such a thing."

"But where are their children, Aisha?"

"I haven't seen them. They must have run." She looked at Dori. "There was a note next to the bodies."

Saeeb was immediately curious. "What did it say?"

Aisha turned to the boy. "Stay away from the Bible people or die."

Despite the note, Dori and her children did not stay away. The next day at church, Dori asked Samar about the killings.

"Samar, why were those people killed? The note said they were Bible people." She pointed a worried look at her friend. "Is your life in danger?"

The clothing room was less crowded today. Samar set her coffee cup gently on the table the two women had set in a corner of the room and smiled softly as she answered. "My dear Dori, this is part of something much bigger than a war in Syria. We are in a battle for souls."

"For souls? What does that mean?"

"Those Bible people you saw were new followers. They loved Jesus so much that they were willing to . . . help others find the truth. The reason for their deaths is the meetings."

"The meetings?"

"All the Bible people have them. Their doors are always open for people who wonder—even in the middle of the night."

Samar paused and tapped on the handle of her coffee cup. "Dori, Sunni Muslims like you have many questions. They wonder, 'How can Muslims be killing other Muslims in this war? Isn't this a fight against Bashar al-Assad and the Alawites?' But when they come to Jordan and meet the Bible people, the hate is gone. As you've already seen for yourself, these people simply love them. Unfortunately, your neighbors were discovered. I know who they were. Someone—we're not sure who—was spying on them, listening to their conversations from outside their window."

Samar closed her eyes before continuing. "Dori, I hope you didn't see the bodies. The murders were brutal. Our friends were decapitated."

Dori grimaced. "Just because they love us?"

"Yes. But there was also another reason. They were refugees and used to be Sunni Muslims themselves. That was before Jesus came to them. God has used them to share the light with many."

"You mean there are other Muslims living in the refugee apartments who now say they are Bible people?"

"Well, yes, Dori. Actually there are many, but the Fundamentalists are looking for them and plan to kill all of them."

"Samar, how can you tell if someone has become a Bible person?"

Samar looked at her friend. "That's simple, Dori. You can see it in their faces. The love in their eyes will tell you."

Over the next week, Dori thought often of Samar's words—and her eyes. For several hours each night after Hania and Saeeb were asleep, she also read the Bible Samar had given her. Then, when Dori slept, Jesus was often there to greet her in dreams.

By the middle of the week after her talk with Samar, the words, the Bible, and the dreams were especially helpful when Hassan called to tell Dori that Rafiq was dead. She grieved deeply, realizing she still thought of her husband as a source of security.

It had been a week since their last conversation at the church when Dori awoke just after sunrise, the pain of her loss burning in her chest. She sat on the floor and gazed at her sleeping children. After several minutes, she reached for her cell phone an arm's length away on the concrete surface, flicked it on, found Samar's number, and called.

"Samar, I'm sorry to call you so early this morning, but I read in Isaiah last night that the Lord binds up the brokenhearted and sets the prisoners free. In Luke, Jesus also said this was why He came." Dori choked with emotion.

"I'm brokenhearted, Samar. And Jesus keeps coming to me in dreams at night. Why does He love me? I'm just a refugee—and now a widow. Why would He care?"

"Dori, come see me today."


While Saeeb and Hania talked with several newcomers at the church, Dori and Samar met in a small room just off the clothing area. Three cups of Arabic coffee later, Samar finished the story about her own conversion. Then she reminded Dori of

Jesus' story—the *real* one, about His death and resurrection, not the one Muslims teach.

Dori folded her hands in her lap. She responded simply, "I'm ready. I love Jesus and want to follow Him."

"Dori, this could cost you your life."

"That's why I've waited so long. I wanted to make sure. This started on the way to Jordan when I saw what happened to our friends the Husseins. The two of them had been more religious, more fervent, more committed to Islam than anyone I had known. When I saw their bodies, I knew they had to have discovered something incredible. Now, Samar, I at least know that if I die, I have found the truth—and forgiveness for all that I've done. Jesus *is* the way!"

A few nights after that, the Hadads' food ran out. Saeeb grumbled, and Hania cried quietly as they lay on the cold cement floor and tried to sleep. Dori stared at the ceiling and said nothing, but an idea formed in her mind. *I'm a Bible person now. I think I know what to do.* She closed her eyes. *Jesus, we are so tired and hungry. We have nothing in this apartment. It's a miserable life, but I know You love us . . .* She felt peace seep into her troubled heart, and, not knowing quite how to conclude her prayer, Dori simply drifted off to sleep.

Sometime in the hours that followed, she had the most remarkable Jesus dream yet. She saw *Him* sitting on the throne, smiling. Brilliant white hair adorned His head, and He looked straight at Dori with intense, loving eyes.

*"I am the King of the universe," He told her, "and, Dori, you are my daughter now. I will take care of you. I have heard your cry."*

Sun shone in the sole window of the apartment living room when a loud knock startled Dori awake. *Not another married man who wants to "help" me.* Dori groaned at the first thought that jumped into her mind.

Saeeb was already up and answered the door quickly.

A deliveryman stood at the entrance with several bags of groceries. From the living room, Dori asked who had sent him.

"I'm not exactly sure who it was. I lost the list of refugees today. But someone that passed me in the alley pointed here and said, 'Go to that apartment.' So here I am." He scanned the interior. "Do you need food?"

For a week, each morning began with a knock at the door. On day two, there were clothes. Then beds and blankets, coats and jackets, even space heaters. No two deliverymen were the same, and none were exactly sure how they had ended up at Dori's apartment.

After seven days, Dori had a fully furnished apartment. And her refrigerator was stocked full.

## A MESSAGE FROM DORI

I have to be discreet when I talk to people about Jesus. I want so badly for them to know Him, though, that I have told many about Him—probably too many. It's not overly dramatic to say that I may end up on a gurney like my neighbors did.

Yet the danger is worth every threatening look. My Hania is now a follower, too. She often prays, "Jesus, I love You *too* much!" It's her way of overflowing in gratitude toward her Savior. I'm grateful that my dear Hania is becoming a woman of God even though she knows the risks as well as I do.

So far, Saeeb is another story. He has seen the difference in our lives but feels as if he is disrespecting the memory of his father by even talking about Jesus. He knows his father was not a truly practicing Muslim, but it's still hard for him.

Fortunately, Saeeb has some friends who love Jesus. He met them at Samar's church, and we still go there every week. Most of the families are Muslims, but some are secret believers. We welcome the new refugees, talk about our days in Syria, and eat like royalty.

Saeeb plays soccer with the boys, and they're like madmen when they cheer for Ricardo Kaka of Milan. Muslims and Christians alike love this man. He is a believer, and one day he scored a goal and then ripped his uniform open. There it was for everyone to see on his undershirt: *I Love Jesus!*

While my life in Jordan will never be what it was in Damascus, I would not go back for all the gold we once had. We were unhappy people surrounded by unhappy people. When you see the cruelty, vicious anger, and bitterness of those who are far from Jesus, their threats of physical violence pale in comparison to the peace our Lord gives so generously.

Jesus and His early followers are also wonderful examples

for us refugees. On the night He was betrayed, He said, "Now is your time of grief, but I will see you again and you will rejoice, and no one will take away your joy" (John 16:22). His followers would soon be forced to leave Jerusalem, making them refugees.

People now tell *me* that I have eyes filled with hope and joy. I no longer have to worry about anything in this life—nothing! Jesus is on the throne, and He watches over me. Whatever happens to me—even if it is persecution and death—must go through Jesus first.

I still ask Him to meet our needs because we are children of the King of the universe and must never expect anything except that Jesus is fully able to provide. Regardless of how good or bad your situation, He is your Provider and will give you what He knows is best for you. You see, when you are in Jesus, you can never be a refugee. You are not forgotten.

Finally, when you think of it, please pray for Saeeb. Hania and I are excited to tell you something: he's been having dreams.

# CHAPTER FOUR

# GET YOUR BIBLE AT THE MOSUL MOSQUE

*I THOUGHT THE Leaning Tower of Pisa was in Italy.*

Shukri Hananiyah shielded his eyes from the sun and chuckled at the nearly nine-hundred-year-old Al-Habda Minaret of the Great Mosque of al-Nuri in Mosul, Iraq. Curved precariously from just above the base to the tip as if blown by a permanent southerly wind, the 150-foot protrusion poked a half dozen bands of barely different shades of beige into the blinding daylight and ended in a cupola roof the color of a bone dried for centuries in the desert sun. For at least a minute, Shukri simply stood staring at the bent tower.

"That thing looks like a banana," he said out loud to no one.

An imam walked by, and without stopping, broke into Shukri's conversation with himself, offering what must have

75

been the standard explanation. "The minaret is bowing to the prophet Muhammad!"

*Is he serious?* Shukri was afraid the cleric was and restrained further comment until the man was safely several feet way. "That's about the worst excuse I've ever heard for bad engineering," he muttered.

While this may have been Shukri's first view of the legendary spire, he knew it would not be his last. He was in Mosul on assignment. God had assured him several weeks ago that the time in his hometown, Fallujah, was over and had been clear that he and his precious wife, Khadija, would relocate to Mosul to bring God's message to that city. For the next month, he planned to walk the area, pray over it, and fast in preparation for their move. Despite the joy he felt at such an explicit calling on what to do next, Shukri also bore the sobering reality that this new direction would bring very different lessons than the life he would be leaving behind.

A handful of years ago, Shukri was the life of every party. Despite terrorism, war, and the violence of life in Fallujah, Shukri maintained his reputation for being a comedian.

"We Iraqis are crazy," he once chattered at an NGO* worker he met in a café. "We didn't like living under Saddam Hussein. We hated him, of course. But you've got to give him credit. There was order, there were rules, and there were consequences—big-time!—for anyone who violated his policies and regulations."

---

* Nongovernmental organization

The newcomer to Iraq nodded and smiled, amused at Shukri's candor.

Glad to have an audience, Shukri continued. "We need that because we Iraqis are an unruly people—always have been! To be completely honest, I think if Fallujah were wiped off the map, Iraq would be a much safer place—just get rid of the whole lot of people who live here. I ought to know. I've been in Fallujah all my life."

The NGO thought Shukri sounded more like an Iranian than an Iraqi.

If his too-honest opinions didn't raise a chuckle among his listeners, Shukri spiced up conversations with a seemingly endless supply of political jokes. He was addicted to other people's laughter and considered it a key to his own survival in the vile life of Baghdad's neighboring city.

Others appreciated the survival technique, too. Shukri made instant friends with everyone he met, and even his wife was astounded by the countless acquaintances clamoring to be near her husband. In a country where religious hatred influences every segment of society, Shukri hated no one—Muslim or Christian, Sunni or Shia, fundamentalist or secular. He prided himself on being able to develop a friendship with anyone. And he received rave reviews from his companions:

- "Shukri! Ah, I've never met anyone quite like him. If he'd ever had an audience with Saddam Hussein, the dictator would have been on the floor, laughing."
- "Shukri would make a great politician. Everyone—and I mean everyone!—loves him."

The entertaining Iraqi maintained his balance in religious matters by assuming God was irrelevant to him personally. Faith in God was an absurdity. After all, how well had it worked out for his country? As far as Shukri was concerned, the Middle East stayed at war because of religion. "Faith" prompted the very terrorist acts that made life so unbearable. Even many of Saddam Hussein's murders were committed in the name of religion. And the Iraqis' *one* country was an illusion.

Thanks to the people of God, three religious cultures fractured every attempt at union. Sunnis, Shiites, and Kurds. Muslims killing Muslims by the thousands infected the once-great Babylonian people. And to prove what? Which one followed the Quran most literally? Or who loves the Prophet Muhammad more? He nearly gagged at the thought.

Shukri kept his real convictions so much to himself that, for years, he convinced even Khadija he was among "the faithful." A Muslim at heart, she finally confronted her husband one day: "You don't believe in Islam anymore, do you?"

Shukri wasn't actually sure he had ever believed it. But whatever shade of conviction he might have harbored—and the myriad friendships it allowed him—changed one night at Omar's house.

The good friend had invited Shukri to his home. Although Shukri had known Omar longer than he could remember, he realized he had never visited his comrade's house. Assuming that Omar recognized the oddity of this lack of hospitality, Shukri figured dinner and an evening with the family was the only agenda. But it was not.

Shukri later explained to some new friends what happened.

I stepped into his house and into a crowd of two dozen smiling people.

"Omar," I asked, "What is this about?"

I was pretty sure I'd just walked into an underground prayer meeting.

"Please, Shukri, stay for just a few minutes and meet my friends."

Despite Omar's plea, my instinct was to walk out as fast as I came in. But as my stomach twisted in knots, something held me there. I've been to mosques—and even a few churches—where people just go through the motions of their religion. They put in their time, like punching the clock at work.

What held me at Omar's house, though, was that these people were not faking it. They might have been really stupid to hold a Christian worship meeting in Fallujah, but they were certainly sincere. Doing this could get them killed. People just don't risk death for something they don't think is real.

So I stayed.

I had never been so loved and welcomed by a group of people as I was at that prayer meeting. Folks I didn't even know were concerned about my family: How were we holding up with all the violence that puts our city on the news night after night? Do we need anything?

Yet no one pressured me to "become one of them." They

just cared about me. One guy, though, pushed me over the top with a particular question: "If you could ask God for anything, what would it be?"

My first thought was that I didn't feel worthy of asking God for anything—especially since I didn't any longer believe He exists. How big an insult is *that*?

But the question remained on the table. "Shukri, we're not asking you to believe like we do. But *if* you believed in God, what would you ask Him for?"

I thought for a minute and then mumbled out the best-sounding thing I could come up with. "I guess if I did happen to believe in God and could ask Him for something, I would ask Him to bring peace to Iraq."

The guy nodded at my answer. "Peace in Iraq would be welcomed by just about everyone on the planet!"

It made me feel good that he approved of my answer, but then he hit me with another version of the question. "Shukri, that's great to want what's good for the country, but if you could ask one thing for *yourself*, what would it be?"

I wondered if this was some kind of genie-in-the-bottle, make-three-wishes test, but then I realized he was dead serious. The honest answer dawned on me, and I almost choked on my reply. "I would ask God to show me how to pray like you pray." I scanned the faces looking at me and nodded. "That's what I would ask." All I could do then was look at the floor.

When I looked up again, all the men and women in the room had pointed their hands toward me and were praying with a fervor I'd never heard before. It was like they really thought someone was paying attention to their prayers—and to me! In a nation where it's hard to believe in anything anymore, *they* believed with all their hearts that God would answer my request.

As tears dribbled down my cheeks, the people closest to me put their hands on my shoulders. With that I simply broke down and sobbed.

When they finished praying (and I finished crying), I noticed something remarkable I'd missed when I entered. Men and women from Muslim and Christian backgrounds were both praying for me. And it didn't seem to have anything at all to do with *religion*. All they talked about was Jesus. That night when I got home, I had a lot to talk with Khadija about.

"Khadija?" Shukri sat down gently on the edge of the bed. "Are you still awake? My dear Khadija, we must talk."

A soft form under the sheets shifted toward him. "Yes. I'm awake. But, Shukri, it's past midnight. Can't it wait until morning?"

Shukri placed a loving hand on the curve of his wife's hip. "No, my sweet wife, it can't. Please: just one cup of tea together and then we can sleep. Okay?"

"One cup?"

"One cup. But first, you must promise that you will not tell me I've gone crazy."

Khadija propped herself on one elbow, cocked her head at Shukri, and smiled. "I'll try." She was always ready to be amused at her light-hearted husband.

As Khadija raised tea to her lips, Shukri set his cup down and looked across the kitchen table at his wife. The glow of the stove light a few feet away created shadows that emphasized the depth of her eyes. "Khadija, would you be willing to *die* for Allah?"

The young woman blinked and pulled her head back from the teacup from which she was about to take a sip. "What?" She didn't think her comical husband was joking.

Shukri pursed his lips and glanced at his tea, and then back at Khadija's face. "Okay. Let me ask my question a different way: How do you know Islam is true?"

Khadija and Shukri talked way past one cup of tea. Sunlight peered through the kitchen window and found their conversation still in progress.

Shukri's question released a flood of inquiries from Khadija: "Do you think Islam is not true? How else would we know the truth if not through Islam? Do you doubt Allah? The imams? The Quran itself?"

Each time, Shukri countered with his best estimate of the answers in light of his experience at the Christian prayer meeting. He wasn't sure what it all meant, but his heart told him there was something worth finding out about in what he'd seen at Omar's house. By morning light, though, Khadija still believed the way to find the answers was not to give up on Islam but to become more committed in hopes of reaching a new level of understanding. Finally, the husband and wife agreed on a plan.

"Khadija," Shukri suggested, "I have a New Testament. Let's read it together."

Khadija stifled the inclination to ask where he'd gotten a

Christian Bible and instead simply agreed to Shukri's idea. Both also decided that extreme discretion was required. They would say absolutely nothing to anyone about this search for truth.


Two weeks later, Khadija joined Shukri at the prayer meeting. Since it was her first time, one of the participants posed a question: "Khadija, if you could ask God for anything . . ."

After that, Jesus began paying visits to the Hananiyah household. One night after completing her reading of the gospel of Matthew with Shukri, Khadija saw Jesus in a dream, resurrected from the dead and fully alive. And the night after reading from John, Jesus introduced Himself to Shukri in a dream as the Good Shepherd. And each morning after the nighttime visits, Shukri and Khadija discovered they had each had the exact *same* dream.


Shukri often repeated the sequence of events that happened next to whoever wanted to hear his story.

> I'm the one who doubted everything when it came to religion, faith, and God, not Khadija. I considered religion a sort of poison. After all, look at the Middle East. It's unraveling once again because religion seems to always cozy up to politics. The result tends to prove the truth of the saying around here that "when you mix religion and politics, you get politics." *Bad* politics, I might add.

Yet Jesus had nothing to do with religious systems *or* politics. He established His authority in the hearts of people every time He opened His mouth: "You've heard it said, but I say to you . . ." Wow! What masterful words! The people could not get enough of what He had to say. The religious leaders were afraid of Him, and rightly so.

In fact, the first time I read the New Testament, I thought the Pharisees were Muslims. They resembled our sheikhs and imams to a tee!

Iraq is known as one of the most corrupt countries in the region, and that is nowhere more obvious than in our religion. As Muslims, we are not supposed to drink alcohol, for example. Yet at most weddings I go to in Baghdad, there's a bar. And how does that happen? That's the funny part. For a price, an imam will waive this particular Islamic standard. All of a sudden, it's okay to drink on that particular occasion. People are glad to oblige, but they can see through the hypocrisy, just like the "real" people did in Jesus' day.

For years, the world suspected that Saddam stockpiled weapons of mass destruction. Although no one seems to have been able to prove it, I think he had WMDs and sent them to Syria. Whether he did or not, we face a far greater threat that I call weapons of mass *deception*. Religion—especially Islam—deceives people into thinking they can get right with God through keeping rules and laws. This idea, of course, is straight from the enemy. His deception is more destructive than bombs because his weapons destroy people for eternity.

When Khadija and I became Jesus followers, we knew immediately we were called to take the message of grace and forgiveness to Muslims. We prayed and fasted, asking the Lord where He wanted to send us. In thirty days, we had our answer: "Go to Mosul" is what we knew God was saying to us.

At first, we were thrilled simply to have a clear direction. Then the reality of our calling began to sink in. Mosul is the ancient city once called *Nineveh*. Jonah chose to run from God rather than obey the call to go there. Now I could understand what he must have felt. For centuries, the Ninevites had earned a reputation as the most brutal regime anywhere. The prophet Nahum had also brought a message of "repent or else" to the Ninevites, which worked for a while. But they quickly returned to their treachery. They killed, tortured, and maimed men, women, and children—and bragged about it. They were even known to skin people alive! Others so feared the Ninevites that sometimes entire villages committed suicide once they found out Ninevites were headed their way.

Today, Islamic terrorists who rule this ancient city carry on the legacy. The parallels are hard to ignore. The same ancient strongholds have gripped the people there since before Jonah's time. Mosul would be no vacation; that's for sure.

Even getting there could kill us. Although the distance from Fallujah to Mosul is less than three hundred miles, any one of the dozens of checkpoints along the way can erupt into a war zone in an instant if the wrong people point guns at each other. There's a bloodbath at one of them nearly every day. Iraqi military controls the checkpoints, but multiple terrorist groups take turns trying to overrun the positions. Suicide bomb trucks are the usual weapon of choice.

Travel from Fallujah to Mosul skirts the western edge of the Sunni Triangle. The boundary stretches from Baghdad in the southeast to Ramadi at the southwest corner and up to Tikrit in the north. Most everyone in this heavily populated area is Sunni Muslim, and each of the cities is among the most violent places in the world. Some geopolitical analysts think the Triangle should become one of three nations within Iraq just for the sake of survival. They doubt that *one* Iraq has a future. The three countries would be based on religion, ethnicity, and political interests: one for the Kurds, one for the Shiites, and one for the Sunnis. The heart of "Sunnistan" would be the Triangle.

Much of the road from Fallujah to Mosul runs along the Tigris River. The tree cover and twists and turns make it impossible for Iraqi security forces to root out the tribal groups that wreak havoc along this ancient water channel. Even so, I was not concerned about traveling alone to Mosul for my month of prayer-walking around the city. I had enough contacts and family friends between Fallujah and Mosul that I could get hourly updates about danger spots if I needed to. It also meant I had places to hide and friends to call along the way in case of emergency.

But thinking about taking my dear Khadija and two children terrified me for their sakes. How could I ever live with myself if one of them were killed on the journey? Concern for my family presented a serious challenge to my fairly young faith. Ultimately, the only thing I could do was trust God for the trip and whatever else happened after that.

Three months after Shukri first mused over the bent mosque tower in Mosul, the headlights of his 1992 Toyota Crown tunneled through the darkness along the outskirts of Fallujah and stared ahead toward Baghdad. Inside, Khadija's forward gaze paralleled her husband's, alert for hints there might be trouble ahead. The road *felt* dangerous. Behind them, Sarah's small left hand stretched across the backseat and gripped the even smaller hand of her brother, Walid. At Baghdad, the family turned north on Route 2. A miraculous calm settled upon the car and its occupants as they steered toward Mosul.

Two hundred miles north, a lone traveler headed onto the Mosul highway to cover the much smaller distance from Erbil to *Nineveh*. Ibrahim al-Medina, though, would be walking this journey for which he had *not* volunteered. The unmarried Arab became a *persona non grata* the instant the Kurdistan government banned all single Arab men under the age of thirty from the region. The law had passed easily and was implemented within a week.

As with most other ethnic pockets of the Middle East, Kurds make no attempt to be politically correct. Profiling is a national pastime, and a single Arab man in a Kurdish-dominated area is considered a guaranteed source of trouble.

Ibrahim's shoulders drooped as the Kurdish guard waved

him through the final checkpoint out of town. As Ibrahim stepped into the Sunni Triangle, he hoped his secret would not be revealed, at least until he could find a safe place to relocate. A believer of only eleven months, Ibrahim's heart ached at the thought of leaving behind the house church that had become his family over the past year. His passion for telling people at his Costa Coffee hangout about Jesus may now be his undoing. He had shared his conversion story with anyone who would listen, and within a few months, his apartment filled to capacity with seekers hungry for his Creation-to-Christ Bible study.

Three nights a week, Kurdish Muslims seeking spiritual fulfillment challenged Ibrahim with questions about the Bible, Jesus, and Christianity in general, but those days were over. With only twenty-six miles separating Erbil from Mosul, Ibrahim reasoned that the news of his conversion had easily reached his family. If he was right, the reunion with his father, a ranking member of ISIS*, would not go well.

Despite the distance that had separated the two believers—and the fact that they had never met—both Ibrahim and Shukri recognized the abysmal spiritual climate they would face as Christians in Mosul. They also knew the uniquely precarious nature of their own status as Christians. Most believers in the area were born into their faith. That brought a modicum of tolerance from virulent Muslim neighbors. The two modern-day Jonahs, though, were *former* Muslims who voluntarily left the faith to follow Jesus. This one fact elevated the threat level

---

* Islamic State of Iraq and Syria

to their safety a hundredfold. Their spiritual defection was an unpardonable slap in the face of Islam.

Yet unlike Jonah, once God made His plan clear, Shukri and Ibrahim bore straight for Mosul. Neither would need convincing in the belly of a whale to do as they'd been told.

An all-night drive from Fallujah and an overnight walk from Erbil brought the two evangelists to Mosul by daybreak. Ibrahim knew of one friend he could trust, and he would risk interrupting Ishmael's breakfast to find out what awaited him in the city.

"Of course they know, Ibrahim!"

Ishmael scowled at Ibrahim across the kitchen table. "It happened about a year ago, right? You know that I care nothing about religion, and it doesn't matter to me, my friend. You can think, believe, or do whatever you want for all I care. But your father does not see it that way. You know that as well as I do!"

Ibrahim stirred his tea and watched the liquid swirl in his cup.

"Ibrahim!"

The visitor's head jerked up at the harshness of his friend's voice.

"Your father has vowed that the day you set foot in Mosul will be your last."

Ibrahim sucked air slowly through his teeth. The filling of his lungs relaxed him enough to subdue panic.

"Go *anywhere* but Mosul, for the sake of whatever God you think you serve! And go now!"

Since the first grade, Ibrahim had loved no friend more than the man who now sat three feet away, pleading with him to leave. He did not take Ishmael's grave concern lightly.

"All right, Ishmael, I'll go somewhere else. And, thank you. You are closer to me than my own flesh and blood." Ibrahim set his spoon on the table. "Let me use the restroom, and then I'll be gone."

Five minutes later, in the upstairs bathroom, Ibrahim froze, hands still pressing a drying towel to his face. The crackle of wood told Ibrahim that the frame had splintered as at least three men crashed through Ishmael's front door. He could tell a struggle was now taking place in the room just below, but he could not see the six-inch knife threatening to slash Ishmael's throat. A man roared at Ishmael, demanding to know the whereabouts of Ibrahim. It was *his father's voice*.

"Yes. I admit he was here." Ishmael gasped out the words. "But he left and headed downtown."

As Ibrahim prayed that his father would believe Ishmael's lie, he set the towel on the bathroom counter and reached for the window. He inched it open, then slipped out noiselessly onto the roof. In three silent steps, he reached the edge and jumped into the backyard. He sprinted away from the house and launched himself over the fence. By the time his father stormed out Ishmael's front door, Ibrahim had disappeared into the neighborhood. But he was not headed for downtown Mosul.

"*Marhaba**, Mother."

Nadimah al-Medina whirled toward the voice. She had not heard her son creep in the kitchen door.

"Mother, I've missed you so much!"

Color drained from the woman's face. "Your father will be here any minute, Ibrahim," she whispered. "You can still run."

"I know, my sweet mother." Ibrahim held out his arms and stepped toward the woman. "And thank you for the warning. But I have come to tell you, Father, and my brothers and sisters the truth. You all must know this."

Nadimah shook her head and extended her right arm to block the hug. "No, Ibrahim, no. Please go."

Before Ibrahim could answer, mother and son heard the front door open. In six heavy steps, Jihad al-Medina appeared behind his wife and scowled at his son. Ibrahim saw the room as a no-man's land between lines of battle. For a dozen seconds, the two men stared at each other across the deadly space.

"Father, if you kill me, I will have completed my holy pilgrimage. God sent me here to bring you the truth. You are the family I love—nothing can change that. But it is Jesus who has set me free." Ibrahim saw the elder man grimace at the word *Jesus*. "I'm not afraid to die."

Jihad al-Medina regarded his son without emotion. "We will see if that is true."

Within an hour, Ibrahim knelt in the intersection by the northwest corner of the Al-Nabi Yunus Mosque; hands duct-taped

---

* An Arabic greeting.

harshly behind his back and tinged blue from lack of circula-
tion. Thirty or so onlookers from the mosque joined Ibrahim's
extended family in a raucous circle around the solitary Christian.
One of the men who had invaded Ishmael's house in the search
for the man now in the street before them wrapped a black blind-
fold over Ibrahim's eyes.

"Jesus," Ibrahim mouthed the word he had come to love
more than any other, "forgive my family. Forgive these people.
Please show them mercy."

Jihad al-Medina touched the muzzle of his AK-47 to
Ibrahim's forehead and spattered the mob with his son's head.

Six blocks west, a Toyota drove slowly along the Al Jamahiriya
Road bridge over the Tigris River. Another messenger of God
had arrived in Nineveh.

More than twenty-seven hundred years had passed since
Jonah reached the banks of the great river, yet the evil of the
early Ninevites still thrived under the command of ISIS, the
new regional, more vicious incarnation of al-Qaeda. Formed by
Abu Bakr al-Baghdadi of Iraq in the spring of 2013, the terrorist
group quickly earned a reputation for brutality so extreme that
al-Qaeda itself disavowed any connection with the organization.
Shukri had heard that the ISIS torture methods were unthinkable even by Middle East standards.

"Shukri, the Lord is giving us favor." Khadija looked at her
husband as he studied the traffic ahead. Sarah and Walid still
dozed in the backseat. "How else can you explain that we've

made it to Mosul without a single problem at any of the checkpoints? The children slept all night, and we are where the Lord has called us to live!"

Shukri sensed the same blessing within the confines of the family car. Outside, though, he sensed only fear and hopelessness. The spiritual dissonance he had felt ever since leaving Fallujah the previous evening was magnified here in Mosul.

He guided the car around a crowd chanting in the street outside a mosque. The rabble obscured their view of a partially headless corpse encircled by the disorderly group. Ibrahim al-Medina would never meet his fellow Jonah in this life.

Shukri pointed at the religious edifice as they passed. "I think the best place to engage Muslims in conversation is at a mosque."

Khadija frowned. "It's probably the most dangerous, too, Shukri."

"But this is where the true seekers are, my love. So many fervent and religious people cry out to Allah from here. And, yes, there are many fundamentalist fanatics around, but I talked to the imam at the Great Mosque when I was here before, and he is fine with me handing out Bibles. He lectured me on the holy books of Islam, of course, and assured me that by reading the Bible, 'Muslims will see that the Quran is the ultimate book and be even more convinced of its perfection.'" He smirked at his wife. "He doesn't suspect that I'm no longer a Muslim. I know he'll find out eventually, but I plan to be moved on to the next mosque by that time."

Shukri patted the steering wheel, his enthusiasm for the

mission building. "Just think: the Great Mosque has been a center for Islamic prayer for ten centuries! Mosul is Iraq's "Second City," and that mosque is its spiritual glue. But starting at Friday prayers, people there will be able to find out all about Jesus."

Khadija merely nodded at her cherished husband's joy.

"How privileged we are, Khadija! Following in the footsteps of Jonah and Nahum!" He turned from the road, riveted his eyes on Khadija, and spoke slowly. "No matter what happens, we *must* cling to the fact that *Jesus sent us here.* His plan will unfold before us."

Two days later, hundreds of "the faithful" jammed the thousand-year-old mosque across the Tigris River from the one at which Ibrahim al-Medina had died that Wednesday. His had not been the only violent death in the city that week. Bombings and firefights between ISIS and Iraqi forces left the bodies of ten other young men in the streets. Killing sprees usually added up to packed mosques on Friday.

A few minutes before the start of midday prayers, Shukri Hananiyah hauled three boxes of Arabic Bibles into the Grand Mosque of Mosul. Magnetic personality in full swing, he stood just inside the main door and greeted arrivals as if he were the senior imam himself.

"This is for you." Shukri's smile sparkled as he extended a book to a gray-bearded gentleman.

"Please. Take one." He offered a fiery-looking twentysomething a Bible.

"Here. This is a gift."

Most nodded appreciatively at Shukri's present and walked on, thumbing through the pages. But a half dozen or so men in white dishdashas scowled at him from just inside the mosque and carried on an agitated conversation, obviously about Shukri. One of the men beckoned to several people holding Shukri's Bibles, but just as a small crowd was forming around the dishdashas, the imam's voice echoed through the gaping interior of the sacred building. The group dissipated.

Shukri could hardly believe that the congenial man he had visited on his reconnaissance trip could launch such an acid diatribe against just about every people group in Iraq. He hit all of them, except, of course, the Sunni Muslims.

Several latecomers scurried in, and Shukri passed out the last of his Bibles. He bent over to pick up the empty boxes he had pushed behind the open door and froze at the words he heard from the imam.

"Mosul will soon be 100 percent Sunni Muslim! No one can stand in the way of this holy cleansing of our ancient city! Christians beware! Your days are numbered!"

Shukri decided it was time to go home.



"How did it go at the mosque?" Khadija patted her hands together, relieved to see her husband at the apartment door but added with a touch of apprehension, "Will you go to another one next week?"

Shukri reached for his wife's hands. "My dear Khadija, I

do think the Lord will call some new disciples from the Great Mosque to follow Him. Time will tell, but I saw faces today that spoke of a deep desire to know God personally. That's why they were at the mosque." He smiled at Khadija. "I could tell many of them were thrilled to have a Bible.

"You know Muslims, Khadija. Many are passionate about their faith, but it's misdirected, and they just don't know it. The Great Deceiver has had his way with them so far, but not for much longer."

Husband and wife walked into their kitchen together.

"Thank you, my faithful wife, for staying here and being on your face before the Lord. For me to walk into a mosque like that, your prayer covering was essential. I believe I have one more week at Nur al-Din before I move to another mosque." He raised his right hand toward the ceiling. "I'm also thankful for your work here in the apartments. I'm amazed at how many people you know already. Are the two families from upstairs still coming to dinner tomorrow night?"

"Yes, Shukri, they are." Khadija hesitated. "But I must tell you, I'm not sure it's a good idea for you to stay at the Great Mosque. I have bad feelings about it."

"I know, Khadija. I've sensed something as well. Let's pray this week for a specific direction from God. Regardless of our plans, everything could change overnight. There's talk that ISIS will attempt to take control of Mosul. We should commit to not worry about tomorrow, as Jesus told us in the great sermon. Whatever happens, we'll live fully for Him every single day."

"I agree, Shukri. We should pray. But I'm afraid . . ." The soft-spoken woman glanced at the floor and back at her husband. "I'm afraid that I will soon be a widow."

"I know, Khadija."

The next Friday, Shukri stood in the kitchen doorway and watched for several seconds as his wife prepared their morning tea. She hadn't noticed him.

"Love of my life! Good morning." Khadija brushed a hand across her eyes and smiled softly at Shukri as he continued. "I must talk with you."

She turned and faced her best friend. "Of course."

"The Lord woke me up this morning, and as I was worshipping Him in prayer, I believe He spoke to me." Shukri paused, measuring his wife's reaction. "I felt like the Lord said to me that I am going to see Him today."

Khadija's jaw dropped. "Oh, Shukri, no! I'm not ready for this! We are only in our thirties! I can't bear the thought of losing you." She pressed her hands together and touched them to her chin. "I beg of you: don't go to the Great Mosque today. It's Friday, and the message must mean that you will be killed when you pass out Bibles and tell people about Jesus!"

"But, Khadija, I've been reading in the book of Acts, and God's message to me could also mean that the Lord will appear in power to Muslims there as well. I don't know if I was being told I will be martyred or that Jesus will appear. I could die, but I'm not sure. This could be *the* breakthrough day for Muslims in

Mosul. Remember: for Jonah and Nahum, everything changed in one day when the Lord intervened."

Shukri shook his head. "No, Khadija, I *must* go today. Jesus said we have to take up our crosses and follow Him. If this means I die, then so be it. I will be with Him. And you and Sarah and Walid will be provided for. He will see to it. We know this is right, my beautiful Khadija." He looked softly at his troubled wife. "We do, don't we?"

Khadija reached for Shukri. "Yes, Shukri, I know this. But somehow the truths of these verses are hitting my heart a different way now. I need some time with the Lord this morning." She wrapped her arms around his waist and pressed her head into his right shoulder. "The thought that when you walk out that door, it may be the last time I see you, hug you, gaze at your smile, and hear you laugh . . . I don't know . . . I don't know if I can do this."

Shukri stroked the back of her head. "I know, Khadija. The only way I can bear this is to know that if this is my last day with you, then it will be my first day with Jesus. I love you, my sweet one." He pulled her close. "Let's go play with the children."

Fifteen minutes before the start of Jumu'ah, Shukri again placed himself by the shoe shelf, just inside the main door of the Great Mosque. And as before, his charm enhanced the eagerness of most mosque goers to receive his gift of Bibles. Several stopped for brief conversations, then walked into the *musalla*, chuckling over one of Shukri's well-timed quips. This week, even before the imam ascended the minbar, Shukri's third box of Bibles was empty. All seemed well at the mosque, and nothing felt even remotely threatening.

Shukri waited until the prayer service ended before leaving. He joined the crowd flowing into the street and jostled two blocks south along Al Shaziani Street. He wondered why the Lord had so clearly impressed him with the thought that he would see Jesus today.

Shukri turned right on Nineveh Street. Although the crowd had thinned, there were still too many people around to notice anyone in particular. He had taken fewer than ten steps from the corner when a hand grabbed his shoulder and jerked him backward.

Shukri spun toward the hand. Six men in dishdashas emerged from the flow of people and formed a circle around him. Under three of the dishdashas, Shukri spied the distinctive bulge of AK-47s. He extended his left hand toward the men.

"I believe I saw you last week at the mosque but didn't have a chance to introduce myself." He smiled. "I am a messenger from the Lord Jesus Christ."

The man who had grabbed Shukri pulled a *janbiya* from under his garment. Sunlight flared off the blade, and the man smiled back. "We are from ISIS."

## A MESSAGE FROM KHADIJA

When the news of Shukri's torture and killing reached me, I was completely numb for about an hour. How could I fight against the will of God? He sent Shukri and me to Mosul to bring the fragrance of Christ to this dark and evil city. As we had prayed, we reasoned that we would be martyred for our glorious Lord someday, and it would be an honor. But now that Shukri was really gone, it did not feel so honorable.

I share these words several months after I lost my beloved Shukri. I am not sure I would have been able to compose myself and voice my feelings before now. I ache for him. It's hard to put into words how much I miss my husband. He loved me with the love of Christ. And little Sarah and Walid were lost without their loving *abu*! But the Lord's grace is rebuilding their shattered hearts.

Yet, you must know this: We are not leaving. God put us in Iraq, and here is where we will stay. Perhaps you, too, have been called to persist at something God has called you to. I am convinced it is our duty as servants of the Most High to stay, go, or continue doing whatever He says until He tells us otherwise.

I also want you to know that the two couples who came to our home after Shukri's first Friday at the mosque became followers of Jesus. The day they believed, we taught them how to share their faith, and now there are *twenty-three* of us that worship Jesus in the middle of the night. Dangerous? Yes. But many more are interested in knowing our wonderful Savior. They are desperately afraid of ISIS and need the hope the gospel gives them. By staying in Iraq, we show that Jesus is our Protector and that we do not fear the sinister works of men.

ISIS is the most vicious terrorist group, perhaps ever, and

we relocated to Erbil. ISIS gave us choices: convert to Islam, pay the jizya tax, leave, or die. I was ready to go see my Jesus and to see Shukri again, but I thought of the children. So we moved on. The presence of Christ is still needed in Mosul, and, I tell you, we Christians will be back someday.

Shukri was an earthly treasure I will also have in heaven. Meanwhile, there are many things I miss about him. His passion for God comes to mind first. After that . . . well, I loved his jokes! He could make the tension leave any situation by his always-present sense of humor. And I suppose I will miss his continual smile.

The hardest thing to talk about, though, is how cruelly ISIS tortured Shukri before he died. They slashed him with knives all over his body before shooting him at least ten times in the head and chest. They dragged him off and buried him in a patch of sand.

The police called me to the scene to identify Shukri's body, and when I arrived, they had already pulled him out of the shallow grave. They showed me the note ISIS had pinned to Shukri's shirt and told me that when they found him, Shukri's right hand was sticking out of the ground and pointing toward heaven. Only one thing helped me bear the sight of my dear Shukri, sprawled on the ground, bloody, beaten, and lifeless: he was smiling.

# CHAPTER FIVE

# THE JOY OF A BAGHDAD BEATING

TASYIR AWAD CURLED into a fetal position under the covers. At 2:00 a.m., he felt no closer to sleep than he had when he crawled in bed three hours earlier.

*Is today the day my family will finally kill me?* The thought wouldn't leave him.

Tasyir had been "Tassie" since he was born, but the family didn't call him by such an affectionate name anymore. Now he was known only as "Infidel." From their perspective, he understood, the name suited him perfectly. Had he merely doubted the faith of his upbringing, he might have gotten away with simply keeping his views to himself. Even sharing questions with a few close friends would have been safe enough. After all, life in the thoroughly Islamic yet radically violent city of Fallujah, Iraq, was enough to make anyone doubt the overall direction of their common religion.

Tassie had seen more killings firsthand at age twenty-two than most Americans see in a lifetime of watching movies. Always in the crosshairs, Fallujah was the battlefield for Saddam Hussein against the Shiites, against the Americans, against other "coalition" soldiers. Now it hosted daily shootouts between al-Qaeda and ISIS. One conflict after another turned the city into a perennial bloodbath. That was the only life Tassie knew or could even imagine.

Until Jesus paid him a visit.

His path to becoming an infidel and receiving visits from Jesus started at the hand of another infidel. While in high school, Tassie met an American soldier on a house-sweeping mission through the teenager's neighborhood. That particular search for insurgents ended just five houses down from the Awad residence when the warriors from the United States found, overwhelmed, and killed the Muslim extremists.

One "evil American occupier" treated Tassie with such respect and kindness during the hunt that the young man remembered him well. Days later, Tassie ran into Joe America, as he called him, and although Joe didn't have much time to talk, he told Tassie that he had prayed for him and the safety of his family.

"Your family was gracious to us, and they are good people," he had said. "I pray that the Lord of heaven watches out for you and them."

*My enemy prays for me?* Tassie couldn't shake the strange thought. *I'm not sure that anyone prays for me except my mother.*

During their brief encounter, Joe also gave Tassie a pocket-sized Arabic Bible. Holding the little book loosely between his thumb and second finger, the boy felt as if he'd been given a poisonous snake. He barely managed a "thank you."

Tassie intended to throw it in the first garbage can he saw after Joe was out of sight, but as he undressed for bed that night, he realized the gift was still in his pocket. He decided to trash it in the morning but read a little that night to relieve his boredom. The Christian book might even be worth a few laughs. He randomly opened the Bible to a part called "John." The first words he saw astounded him: "I am the light of the world."

That night, the dreams started. A man approached Tassie in a darkened room. The visitor called the boy by name, and instantly light flooded the chamber. *"Tassie, I am the light of the world. I will show you the way. Will you follow Me?"*

No longer garbage, the Bible became Tassie's most valued possession. He devoured every word, desperate to discover what the Bible, the dreams—his life!—meant.

One of his discoveries was a group of Jesus followers. They gathered in late-night meetings, right next door to a mosque. The fellowship even had a name that Tassie took as a sign he was on the right path. They called themselves The Lighthouse.

Several months into daily reading of the New Testament and meeting with his Lighthouse friends, Tassie secretly committed himself to faith in Jesus. But his secret had not remained hidden. Now, three years later, it seemed certain that saying yes to Jesus would soon be saying no to his own life. Today, that reality was frighteningly close. Perhaps it wouldn't matter if he didn't get a good night's sleep. He checked the time again. It was nearly three o'clock.

Fifty miles east, Layla Jabour also lay awake. Agony in the left side of her face prevented sleep. She feared her cheekbone was fractured from the evening's assault by her husband. Life in the streets of Baghdad was nearly intolerable, but inside the Jabour home, it was worse.

"When did your son Abdul begin smoking?" Maha, Layla's friend since childhood, had asked Layla not long ago.

"Abdul doesn't smoke. He's only five years old."

"Then why does he have cigarette burns on his arm?"

"He burned himself by accident."

Layla reviewed the conversation in her mind. She had been embarrassed to tell even her best friend the real reason for the burns. They were from his father, of course, and it was no accident.

*Cruel.* Surely there was a stronger word for Abdullah Jabour than that. He was a man who tortured his wife more thoroughly than guards abuse inmates in Baghdad Central Prison. A father who took pleasure in searing his five-year-old's flesh with the tip of a cigarette. A pervert who numbed his own pain by inflicting it on others. The merciless warden of the Jabour household, Abdullah punished his wife every night for no reason other than that she existed.

Twenty-five years her senior, he had married Layla after serving Saddam Hussein in the Iraq–Iran War from 1980 until

1988. Now sixty, the ruthless former soldier fought his own battle against despair with the prescription pain medications he was entitled to for life, thanks to a serious wound suffered in the glorious victory over Iran.

Even if Layla had not married Abdullah, life in Iraq would have been a nightmare. As long as she could remember, bloodshed in the streets was the norm. From his first day in power, Saddam Hussein designed and produced a culture of fear that paralyzed Iraqis. Then came a nine-year war against Iran that ended with one million people dead. After that, a Saddam-sanctioned genocide exterminated thousands of Kurds in northern Iraq. Gulf War I blurred into Gulf War II. And now, Shiites and Sunnis shred Baghdad day by day in their battle for power, each side trying to outdo the other's atrocities. She wondered if a pile of rubble would be the only thing left of Baghdad when it ended.

In the Baghdad arena, Sunnis and Shiites were the gladiators. In the Jabour house, Layla was the slave, subject to violence that intensified as Shiites exerted greater control in the streets. Abdullah raged against Shiite politics, with Layla as the whipping post. He hated Prime Minister Nouri al-Maliki, but his fists lashed out only at Layla's soft flesh. He believed that all he had suffered during the "great war" was now in vain. The deranged man longed for the days of Saddam Hussein.

The dismal evening routine drained any hope from Layla. Each night, Abdullah forced his wife to sit at his feet and hear "teaching" about politics. And each night, his anger festered until the fall of Iraq to the Shiites became her fault. Tonight, though, had been the worst yet. Abdullah had turned his wrath once again toward Abdul, and Layla had had enough. She offered herself—for even more abuse—in place of her son.

"Abdul is only five years old, Abdullah, and he barely talks. He makes animal sounds because you treat him like an animal. You can beat me. Kill me if you want to, but, please, stay away from Abdul. I will take his beatings."

Abdullah obliged his wife, and Layla Jabour went to bed that night with no hearing in one of her ears. The blow that she feared had broken her cheekbone had sent her reeling to the floor, and in a last act of fury, Abdullah had pinned her down and rammed a metal rod into her right ear. She had felt the eardrum rupture and now heard nothing on that side.

The one mercy in the Jabour home was that Layla and her husband slept in separate rooms. He had collapsed onto his bed after the night's torture session, and now Layla lay on her back alone in the dark. She closed her eyes, the despair in her heart too deep for tears or sleep and spoke softly to perhaps no one.

"God, *where* are You? Where are You! Every night, I plead with You to rescue me. Do You ignore me because I'm a woman? Do You not hear my prayers because of that?"

She stopped and opened her eyes. For several minutes, Layla listened to Abdullah's heavy breathing down the hall. Thankfully, the whimpering from Abdul's room had subsided more than an hour ago, and Layla welcomed the quiet from his direction. Now, as she stared toward the ceiling, a new thought formed in her mind.

"No, God. I will ask another question of You," Layla

whispered to the darkness. "Perhaps I've been asking the wrong thing. Let me try this."

She paused, strangely aware that she felt the need for courage to say the next words. She heard Abdullah snort and raised both of her hands in front of her face, resting them gently across her eyes.

"God, *who* are You? Maybe I've been praying to the wrong God all these years. Is that why You're silent?"

Layla dropped her hands to the bed and glared into the black room. "Help me! I'm crying out to You! Abdul and I cannot leave this horrible man, or we will starve on the streets of Baghdad. *Who* . . . are . . . You?"

As she breathed out the three last words, exhaustion engulfed Layla's body. Her conversation with the empty room ended abruptly in sleep. But in the middle of the night . . .

*"Layla! I am Jesus. I'm here now, and I will defend you and Abdul. Your days of weeping will soon be over."*

That's all the man said, and then He was gone. But Layla would never forget the dream.

"We've already announced your death, Taysir. You must leave."

By 5:00 a.m., Tassie had finally dozed. Now, sitting at breakfast across the table from his father, he struggled to absorb the words. The older man sat straight, left hand spread flat on the table next to his coffee cup. His eyes narrowed.

"Tassie, my son, leave Fallujah. Please." Anger and sorrow battled in the man's voice. "You can never come back, or we will likely *all* be killed. I do not agree with you and this other religion *you* now believe, but I'm not even sure about *our* religion anymore. I do know that for you, staying here means death." His eyes searched for a place to look. "Today."

Tassie watched his father's discomfort, unable to feel any emotion. This wasn't real.

Maher Awad balled his hand into a fist and stared at it resting on the table. "We may never see you again," he said at last. "But go now, before our relatives arrive to celebrate your execution."

The two men sat in silence, each avoiding the other's eyes. After several minutes, Tassie Awad stood abruptly and spoke softly to Maher. "*Shukran**, Father."

Tassie disappeared into the adjacent family room. His mother, brother, and two sisters rose somberly from their seats as Tassie entered. Good-byes would be swift.

The departing son embraced his mother, then his brother and sisters. Finally, he turned toward his father, who had followed him into the room and bowed slightly in his direction.

"Shukran, Father. Shukran."

Emotion returned and tears dripped down Tassie's cheeks. He touched his father's shoulder as he walked past him and back into the kitchen. "Shukran," he repeated softly as he opened the back door and stepped outside.

---

* *Thank you.* An expression that conveys extreme gratitude.

Five minutes later and half a block up the street from home, Tassie had a plan. He would go to the best place he could think of to blend in and disappear. He raised his right hand and hailed a cab.

"Baghdad, please, sir. To the Umm al-Qura Mosque."


For two hours, a flood of hurt, confession, anger, and new-found hope poured from Layla. Between sips of tea in her best friend's living room, the broken woman told Maha the real reason for cigarette burns on Abdul's arm, why she so often sported bruises or limped or grimaced in pain when touched. She described the living hell of her husband's political ranting. Nevertheless, Layla's monologue stalled when she reached the part about an unusual dream she had the night before.

"I'm grateful that you've finally felt free to unburden your-self about these things with me, Layla." Maha rested her hand carefully on her friend's knee. "But it seems like there's still something you want to tell me."

Layla sighed and caressed the edge of her teacup with her right index finger. "Yes. There is." She looked up at Maha with a half smile. "I had a revelation last night."

Maha leaned back on the couch. "A revelation?"

"I believe that's what you would call it. I guess with all I've told you so far, I might as well explain this, too." She paused. "Jesus came to me last night in my dreams."

"Jesus?"

"Yes. The prophet—or whatever I should call Him."

"I see." Maha stood up and took two steps to the center of the room. She turned to look at her friend on the couch. "That's very significant. I think it also means that it's my turn to tell you a few things."

Layla's eyes followed Maha as she began slowly pacing.

"I've never lied to you, Layla. But neither have I told you everything that's been going on in my life. Like you, I've had my secrets. Honestly, I was afraid to tell you what is most important to me because I didn't know how you would take it."

Layla smirked. "You're committed now. With a build-up like that, you *have* to tell me."

"Of course." Maha nodded. "Here it goes: Layla, I follow Jesus now." She let the words settle. "In fact, my whole family does. We're all Jesus followers. Christians."

Layla's lips parted. Maha stopped pacing.

"Even your father?"

Maha nodded.

"But he's an *imam*. How can this be?"

"He *used* to be an imam, Layla. Now he gives all his allegiance to Jesus."

Maha walked back to the couch and sat down beside the puzzled woman. "Layla, there are many of us in Baghdad, but we tell no one, of course. You know this city is the vortex of the Sunni–Shiite war. *Both* sides would fight over who gets to kill us for being infidels. Layla, people in Iraq are *sick* of religion, especially in Baghdad. There is another way, though."

"I do very much want to know more."

"Then you must come with me tonight. Our group of

followers meets at 1:00 a.m. You can sneak out of the house and come with me. Abdullah will be asleep by then, and that means Abdul will be safe."

"Tonight? Really?"

"Layla, you *must*."

Less than three miles from the west bank of the Tigris River, the Umm al-Qura Mosque stands tribute to the insanity of Saddam Hussein. While Fallujah on the Euphrates River boasts of being the City of Mosques, the mother of all mosques resides in Baghdad, the second-largest Arab city in the world (only Cairo is larger). Saddam claimed a dubious victory for Iraq against Iran and celebrated by constructing the monstrous and bellicose Umm al-Qura. Four outer minarets built to resemble Kalashnikov rifles extend 141 feet above an artificial lake. Surrounded by the water, four more, slightly shorter, Scud missile–shaped minarets stand guard around the core mosque building.

Yet the structure was built to house an even more bizarre creation inside. Before Saddam's death, a one-of-a-kind Quran drew admirers. Saddam had commissioned this edition of the holy book and had it printed, allegedly, *in his own blood*. No longer on display, the volume had not been universally popular, but its legacy remains attached to the mosque in which it once resided.

After his taxi ride from Fallujah, Tassie mingled with the crowds around Umm al-Qura. He had heard rumors that others like him—infidels—could be found here. By early afternoon, he confirmed those allegations. The Jesus follower he met quickly accepted Tassie's story of conversion and now flight for his life. Apparently, such fleeing was not uncommon. The man invited Tassie to a meeting of believers and even offered that Tassie could share his testimony and whatever else God placed on his heart to tell the group. Relieved that he would not have to wait long to speak about the joy of his faith, Tassie accepted the proposal without hesitating.

An hour after midnight, twenty people crammed into the basement of a house within sight of the Umm al-Qura's weapon-like minarets. Welcoming eyes encouraged the newcomer to begin.

"Tonight, I'm grateful for this chance to speak to you." Tassie pulled a New Testament from his hip pocket and gingerly separated its ragged pages. Three years of fervent daily use had rendered the small book delicate. "The Lord has laid on my heart that we should study Jesus' prayer for His followers the night before His death. If you have a Bible, please open it to John 17."

The young preacher read with passion and transitioned seamlessly to a deeply personal sermon. As he spoke, one particular woman in the audience drew his attention. He felt the pain in her badly bruised face and surmised that her head was cocked to one side so as to better hear his words.

"Jesus was willing to die for us. We must do the same for Him. We live in Baghdad, and this is not far from the ancient city of Babylon." Tassie scanned his listeners. "Did you know that Babylon is mentioned more times in the Bible than any other city except Jerusalem?"

Several in the gathering nodded. A few shook their heads.

"For the most part, Babylon is a symbol of rebellion against God. Isn't that a great way to be known?" Tassie chuckled. "From the Tower of Babel in Genesis, to the last book of the Bible, called Revelation, Babylon is forever associated with *paganism.*

"And Jesus has called us to live in this difficult place. Now, look at what He says in John 17: 'May they be one, just as I and the Father are one.'"

Layla Jabour stared at Tassie's face, her mouth open, mesmerized by this man from Fallujah.

"Each one of you is a miracle. I'm sure you didn't go looking for Jesus." He shrugged his shoulders. "Neither did I. *He* came looking for *me,* and He used many people along the path to draw me. Even an American soldier I'd thought of as a vile enemy reached out to me. I saw Jesus in *him!*

"That He found all of us is beyond wonderful. I know you each know that. But we have a desperate mission, and to complete it, we must remain as one. We cannot survive any other way."

Maha raised her hand toward Tassie. "What is our mission?"

Without blinking, Tassie replied firmly, "To show Baghdad who Jesus is."

Tassie explained what he believed the dangers would be in this mission, but also the rewards. He concluded his talk with a testimony of the Lord's work in his life over the last three years.

After Tassie's message, the group paired off to pray. Maha

and Layla chose a corner of the room and sat together on the floor in silence. Layla sensed Maha was praying and watched her friend for several minutes.

When Maha looked up, Layla spoke. "I've never been so inspired in my life by someone's words. What Tassie said made me cry. And those words he read from the Bible. Each one pierced my heart! I must do something. I must." Her voice trailed off.

"Layla, Jesus sees your heart already. He knows you love Him."

Layla looked startled, but Maha wasn't through.

"Your tears are liquid words," she went on. "He hears you loud and clear and knows you need Him."

For the next three nights, Layla sneaked out of the house to meet Maha and listen to more of Tassie's teachings. At prayer time on the third night, Layla wrapped her hands around Maha's and said, "I'm ready to follow Jesus."

Layla removed her sandals and tiptoed through her back door just before the sun rose over Baghdad. This night had been even better than all the previous ones put together. She could not stop smiling and felt sure her feet never touched the ground as she dressed and climbed into bed. Her life was committed to the wondrous Man in her dreams. Layla's inner world felt as bright as the desert at noon despite the darkness that still shrouded her outer life.

The next night, Abdullah beat her mercilessly.

And the next one after that.

"This is not for Abdul. It's all for you, Layla. Tramp! Where have you been at night? With another man? I should kill you now!" The aging man's still powerful hands squeezed Layla's right forearm till she thought it would snap.

"Abdullah, please. It's not what you think. You wouldn't understand, though." She pressed her left hand over the hands on her captive arm.

"Try me!" Abdullah roared in his wife's face and shoved her into the kitchen wall.

Abdullah stormed past Layla toward the stove as she blurted out the first words of her story. Through his rage, the man heard only the word "dream." Layla leaned against the wall, her back to Abdullah, and sobbed out her story about falling in love with Jesus. The second time Layla spoke the name "Jesus," Abdullah's nostrils flared. He grabbed an iron skillet from the top of the stove and slammed it against the back of Layla's head. The woman lurched to the floor and lay motionless.

Through the week that followed, Abdullah's pitiless brutality continued. He swore at Layla that he would kill Abdul if she tried to convert him, and she knew her husband was serious. Paranoid that his wife and son would leave him, Abdullah took Layla's cell phone and promised to hunt them down and kill them both if they were to escape.

On the morning of the eighth day of her new life, Layla ran for help. The night before, Abdullah had turned once again on their son, and she would not bear seeing Abdul harmed. While Abdullah was at work and the boy was napping, Layla dashed the several blocks to Maha's house. *Maha will know how to help*, she reasoned, *and I can trust her not to tell anyone about my misery at home.*

As Layla reached Maha's yard, she slowed to a walk. Breathing heavily, she puzzled over the scene and slowly approached a group of people lounging in plastic chairs in front of the house. She vaguely recognized a dozen or so of Maha's uncles, cousins, and other extended family members.

A cousin stood up. "Layla?"

"Yes. That's right. I'm a friend of Maha." Layla felt she had intruded on something. "Forgive me. Have I interrupted a family event? Someone's birthday party?"

"So you didn't hear the news? I thought perhaps that's why you were here."

"What news?" Now worried, Layla scanned the somber faces looking at her. "Where's Maha?" She almost yelled the question.

The cousin blinked and said without emotion, "In here." He pointed to the house, then motioned her to follow him.

As the man opened the front door, Layla smelled blood.

"Maha, her husband, and their children were given a death sentence for converting to Christianity, and it was carried out last night." The nearly emotionless voice carried a hint of satisfaction.

From the entrance, Layla could look into the living room. Her hand jerked to her lips as her whole body shuddered. Layla gagged twice.

Dried blood speckled the walls. Several smears ended in bloody handprints. Five severely damaged corpses, arranged in size from large to small, lay on the floor. Layla recognized the second largest as the tortured body of her best friend. Layla had stepped into a nightmare.

"They left our glorious religion!" The voice beside her justified the revolting scene. "You may think this is tragic, but remember, they brought this judgment on themselves."

Layla turned and bolted out the front door. Behind her, the cousin's voice bellowed, "They deserved it!"

Layla ran two blocks before she collapsed onto the sidewalk against a retaining wall and groaned, "How could my life get any worse?"

She leaned her head against the bricks behind her and sobbed. Fortunately, no one else was on the street, and for five minutes, her anguish flowed. When the tears stopped, she simply sat, unmoving, on the ground. After several more minutes, a single word entered her thoughts, a name: *Tassie*. Perhaps he could help her. Or even more important now, perhaps she could help him.

A fast-paced, fifteen-minute walk took her to the Umm al-Qura. As she had hoped, the zealous young preacher was there. She found him alone, standing at the edge of the lake, in the shadow of a Kalashnikov minaret.

"Tassie! You have to leave!"

Tassie startled at the abrupt greeting.

"I know you've been sent from God," Layla continued, "but you've also been given a second chance when your family decided not to perform the honor killing on you. But you're not out of danger—*we're* not out of danger!"

"Yes, Layla, of course I know we're in danger—"

Layla cut him off. "You don't know yet, do you?" She breathed hard over the words she was about to say. "Maha and her family were murdered last night. They were butchered! Tassie, I saw them. It was hideous!"

"God have mercy, Layla!" Wide-eyed, Tassie gaped at the terrified woman.

"I'm sure the fundamentalists know all about you, too, Tassie. Maha and her family were horribly tortured, and one of them must have told the killers about our group. Surely they have your name!"

Tassie raised a calming hand. "But, Layla, Someone else has my name, too. Jesus has written it in the Lamb's Book of Life. I'm ready to die if they come for me. But know this: these murderers will hear the truth. Before they kill me, I will offer them a chance to follow the Light."

Movement at the base of the minaret behind Tassie caught Layla's eye. Over her friend's shoulder, she saw a handful of clerics marching toward them. Tassie saw tears forming in Layla's eyes and turned to see what she was looking at. As Tassie faced the approaching Muslims, Layla dashed into the sunlight and disappeared in a crowd of people walking toward the street.

That night, dinner came and went without any explosions from Abdullah. He offered no political tirades and barely spoke to Layla.

*Does he know about Maha and her family?* Abdullah's odd

passivity worried Layla. *Surely he knows. This sort of news spreads like leaves blowing in the wind. Does he have something in mind for Abdul and me?*

The unusual evening ended with Abdullah in bed early and no new injuries to Layla. She kissed Abdul on the forehead and tucked him in bed. Apparently, he would be safe tonight, too.

She watched her hands wash the dinner dishes while she mulled over the day's events. Although her body was intact tonight, her heart was broken. In one terrible day, she had lost her best friend and confidante—and a dear sister in Christ. She also wondered what became of Tassie after she had abandoned him at the mosque. *Is he still alive? Is he being tortured by the clerics?*

Questions and ghastly images of Maha and her family still played in Layla's thoughts as she attempted to sleep. For two hours, she stared at darkness and listened to the intermittent stirrings of her sleeping son and husband. Once sleep came to Layla, so did a Visitor.

*"Layla! Tonight is the night for you and Abdul to leave!"* Though she heard the voice in her dream, she also knew she should obey. *"Go to Jordan. I have people waiting for you there. Head straight for Amman."*

Waking with the dream voice still in her ears, Layla grabbed as many Iraqi dinars as she could find in Abdullah's stashes around the house. She wrapped her arms around Abdul and carried the sleeping child downstairs and out the front door. She was astounded to find a lone taxi idling at the street corner near her house, almost as if it were waiting for her.

"How close can you take me to the Jordan border?"

The cab driver shrugged. "How much money do you have?"

Her cash offer satisfied the man behind the wheel, and five wearisome hours in the taxi led to five additional aggravating hours in line at the Al-Karama checkpoint.

The Jordanian border guard offered only a terse interview when Layla reached his station. "What is your reason for visiting Jordan?" He shifted his eyes lazily toward Abdul. "And why is your son crying? Is he sick?"

"Yes." Layla straightened her shoulders and continued energetically. "He needs medical care, and we need a break from the chaos in Baghdad. I also hope to see some friends on our visit."

"Hmmm. I see." The man handed the passport back to Layla. "Well, Layla Jabour, welcome to Jordan."


## A MESSAGE FROM LAYLA

I am thankful to the Lord to be alive. Since He allowed me to leave Iraq, my days of deep sorrow are over, and I feel His joy all the time now.

Still, the enemy rages in Iraq. Maha's family remains a model of courage for me. I found out that her father, the former imam, and her mother were held prisoner for days after Maha's death, and then they were martyred too.

Since I have not heard anything about Tassie, I think he is still alive. If so, I suspect he continues talking with people at the mosque and teaching in group meetings. He was very sure of his calling, and I suspect he will continue ministering this way until he dies.

When Abdullah found out I was safe in Jordan, he vowed to come here and take me back to the torture chamber that my house had become. So far, he has not fulfilled this threat.

My sweet Abdul has suffered much and now receives counseling. He's making progress. The hurt buried deep inside made him extremely aggressive when we first came to Amman. He found relief from his own pain by hurting others—much like his father. Now, though, he plays with other children without hitting them.

Pastor Sahar—who works with refugees from Iraq and Syria—said Abdul seemed more animal than human when he met him, but the Lord Jesus is redeeming all of this. Abdul even prays out loud to Jesus. Sometimes he prays too loud, in fact, and I have to make sure our Muslim neighbors don't hear him and tell the imam.

Through all the difficulties of my life—the wars in the streets and the wars in my home—I have learned something from Jesus that has shaped my life. His power cannot be hindered or stopped. Nations may be at war, and ISIS may want to rule the world. Evil is called good, and good evil. But Jesus is the greatest force in the universe. One day, He will judge the nations. He will condemn the government and religious rulers who keep people in fear. They *will* be accountable.

To be honest, this is part of my hope. The brutality and injustice I've seen cry out to be avenged. While a few may come to justice in this life, in the end, Jesus will see that justice is done for all those who have suffered.

Another part of my hope, though, is very real, *here and now.* Over and over, I see Jesus reach down to the hurting, the desperate, and the forgotten, when they cry out to Him. I'm a great example of how He does that. With my simple question of "God, *who* are You?" Jesus came to me. I still have Jesus dreams from time to time. He knows I continue needing encouragement.

His love for me inspires my love for others. He's called me to work among refugees in Jordan who have come from Syria, and it's a difficult calling. To bolster my own commitment, I read the Bible to discover all it has to teach me about Jesus. I memorize scriptures, and the words pierce my heart every time I read them.

The work with Syrian refugees is draining, but I can relate to their pain because of my own. My suffering was not wasted.

When hurting women from Syria invite me into their lives to tell about their anguish, I feel as if I'm standing on holy ground. And Jesus is there, too. He sees, touches, and heals. I am proof of this. So, pray for us who serve Jesus among the Syrian refugees! And pray for a precious sister I've met here who helps many people. She and I pray together every day. You know her, too, a refugee from Syria. Her name is *Dori.*

# CHAPTER SIX

# A BODYGUARD IN
# SAUDI ARABIA

HOVERING A HALF mile above the streets of downtown Dubai, the tip of Burj Khalifa stands nearly twice the height of America's second-tallest building—the Willis Tower in Chicago—and a thousand feet higher than America's newest and loftiest mega-skyscraper, One World Trade Center. From bottom to top, the altitude difference is so extreme that outside temperatures can vary as much as eighteen to twenty degrees Fahrenheit. The edifice crowns a city all but obscure as recently as the 1980s but now ranking as a global destination beside the likes of New York, Tokyo, London, and Paris.

The wildly expanding young city of Dubai resembles a teenager struggling to break free of his past and warrant the attention of peers. "The past" started in AD 630, when Islamic invaders conquered the Arab emirates. Ruling sheikhs could not match the force and aggression of warriors sent by Muhammad himself, and for the sake of self-preservation, residents converted to the new religion.

Under the Muslims, nine emirates busied themselves with day-to-day life on the southeastern end of the Arabian Peninsula. When rule passed to Great Britain in 1892, the power of the sheikhs remained dormant—waiting for the petro-genie to call them onto the world stage. After gaining independence in 1972, the emirates crafted a plan to consolidate as one nation, but Bahrain and Qatar opted out to become their own sovereign states. The remaining seven became the United Arab Emirates.

Sovereignty for the UAE arrived just in time to seize the lavish opportunity awaiting a country swimming in oil. Now, in the twenty-first century, the United Arab Emirates boasts an economy second in the Arab world only to Saudi Arabia, and despite its diminutive size—approximately the area of South Carolina—it is home to the world's seventh-largest reserve of crude oil.

Petroleum opened the door to the imaginations of wealthy Arabs intent on drawing attention—and many, many tourists—to the Emirates. It birthed places like the Palm Islands. As seen from above, this opulent array of man-made landmass depicts palm fronds projecting into the waters along Dubai's coast. Sand dredged from the Persian Gulf created islets large enough to host luxury villas, high-end restaurants, ritzy malls, and more than a hundred hotels. Sightseers from all over the world—and especially less pampered parts of the *Arab* world—flock to Dubai.

On one particular weekend, though, Dubai visitor Mina Karim had not come to the city's Jumeirah Beach to sightsee. She was there to dance and drink—and she had found a place lavish by most standards yet still cheaper than the world's highest nightclub on the 144th floor of the Burj Khalifa. Three miles up the coast from Palm Islands, the Night Club Alibi suited her just fine.

"What happens in Dubai *stays* in Dubai. Agreed, cousin?" She hooked her right arm playfully through her escort's left.

"As always." Hakeem winked at his dark-eyed relative and towed her shapely form onto the dance floor.

Mina Karim loathed the burqa but felt safe shedding hers only while partying in Dubai. At home in Saudi Arabia, covering herself like every other "good Muslim" woman was the only option for outerwear. Yet tonight, even with her midriff fashionably exposed, Mina remained more covered than most other patrons of the club and far more than the duo of topless statues bulging from the wall on either side of the sound booth.

DJ Jack howled between selections of Arab techno rock, adding to the chaos of twentysomethings writhing on the dance floor. Mina relished the frenzied relief from her parents' strictures. To her, visiting cousins in the Emirates was a godsend. At least the idea of visiting relatives who work in Dubai's world-class hotel industry satisfied her mother and father. They could imagine her among protective family members loyal to Islam, and Mina was only too happy to encourage the mental image. Tonight, though, her sole protective cover was an alias—she was Sonja from Spain—meant to obscure any possibility of detection from home while she indulged in all that the Las Vegas of the Middle East had to offer.

"Hakeem!" Mina shouted above the din. "How is it that Dubai is in the UAE, a supposedly strict Islamic country, and yet 'anything goes' here?" She draped arms around her cousin's neck and pulled herself close to his right ear. "I don't get it. I wish Saudi Arabia would loosen up."

"Cousin, don't be so naive." Hakeem's lip curled. "Such things are done in our beloved Saudi Arabia, but they're kept behind closed doors . . . usually closed *and locked* doors," he added with a laugh.

Mina threw her head back and guffawed. She and Hakeem had missed the Alibi's grand opening by a few days, but the scene was still hot enough to celebrate her sensual cravings.

Six hundred miles due east, Rafia Abbar was celebrating, too. Her party was of the far tamer variety to which residents of Riyadh, Saudi Arabia, were accustomed. There would be no dancing and certainly no alcohol, but an enormous spread of Middle Eastern food was offered to a house packed full of relatives and friends.

*Professor* Abbar and her large extended family gathered to honor her promotion at the Imam Islamic University of Riyadh. Her elevation to department chair of Islamic Studies for Women brought with it both heightened prestige *and* salary. Her specialty in sharia law for women once again served her career advancement well. But preoccupation with well-wishers and focus on the party in her home would leave no reason for the university teacher to wonder about the activities that night of one of her students on holiday in the Emirates.

Despite their common involvement at Imam Islamic University, Rafia and Mina were as different as Mecca and Dubai. Rafia's life goal was to teach the Quran, model the *sunnah**, and mold young Muslim women into strict examples of sharia law in action for other Muslims to see and emulate.

Mina hoped one day to live in Dubai, work in the travel industry, and imbibe the good life in every way possible. Islamic standards felt to her like concrete shoes. She had become an expert at making her parents think she was a committed Muslim—or so she thought until they enrolled her at the Imam Islamic University. Perhaps they had begun to suspect that she needed some advanced training.

The semester break couldn't have come too soon for Mina. Even during her licentious getaway, though, she could not quite shake the embarrassment of one of her most recent classroom incidents.

Midway through her first semester, Mina had struggled to keep up even a veneer of motivation. Her grades dropped well below average, and unyielding academic pressure overwhelmed her. Professor Abbar was well on her way to becoming Mina's nemesis.

---

* The practical application of principles taught in the Quran.

"Mina!" She felt the woman's pleasure at underscoring the struggling student's weakness. "Stand up, and recite your memory work from the Quran!"

Mina rose slowly. She had not even looked at her homework, much less memorized it. "I was not feeling well last night, Professor Abbar. I was sick, but I will be prepared tomorrow." Both women knew it was a lie.

"Mina! I am not asking for you to make more excuses! You have already proven yourself a professional at that."

A collective giggle rippled through the class.

"I put up with you every day, but you cannot afford to miss homework if you are going to memorize the Quran! To be *hafiza** takes discipline, and that is a quality you clearly lack!" She stared silently at the student for several seconds, drawing out the shame. "Sit down!"

That night, in her dorm room, Mina laid awake, listening to the steady breathing of her roommate. *She always sleeps so well.* Mina was fairly sure she did not like the woman with whom she lived. *And she always does her homework.*

Mina's thoughts shifted to her own unhappiness. How would she ever memorize the Quran when reading it was hard labor? She detested *the book*. She longed for her coming escape to Dubai—however temporary.

The last of the party guests had kept Rafia and her husband

---

* A woman who has memorized the entire Quran.

up far too late. Ismail was already sleeping beside her when the professor finished her reading of the suras and kissed Ismail softly on the forehead. She reached for the bedside lamp and clicked off the light.

Rafia closed her eyes, expecting to fall asleep quickly, but instead, the image of her poorest student flashed into her mind. Despite the girl's contempt for study, Rafia actually liked Mina. She chuckled over the young woman's recent attempts to get out of doing homework. *One day,* Rafia thought, *Mina just might understand what this is all about, and when she does, she may become a great teacher herself.* She laughed again, quietly. *Someday.*

"Jesus!" Rafia jolted herself awake and sat up.

Her groggy husband opened one eye. "*What* did you yell? *Jesus?*"

"Ismail, I'm not sure what happened. I was dreaming. A man in a white robe called me and said His name was . . ." Rafia realized she was explaining to herself. Ismail had already fallen back to sleep.

Rafia lay back down, but as soon as she was asleep again, the man in the white robe came back.

*"Rafia, I love you. I am Jesus."*

The next week, Rafia's Jesus dream still puzzled her, but students had returned, and there was not much time to ponder the odd nighttime event.

"Professor Abbar, I have my homework completed today."

Mina had read her Quran lesson for the whole flight home from Dubai, although not just for the sake of pleasing Rafia Abbar. The reading helped her disengage from the delight she had felt while in the UAE and prepare for her morose life back home. That, and she assumed it made her look especially respectable to fellow passengers.

Mina stood and recited her suras, but not as smoothly as she had planned. Professor Abbar had expected Mina to fail, and the girl did not disappoint her. Nevertheless, she saw that the beleaguered student had put forth some genuine effort and chided her more gently than usual.

"You're still going to have to work a little harder, Mina. Remember: you are not memorizing the Quran to get your degree. You are memorizing it so it will guide you in the path for your life. This is your *foundation*." The professor paused and scanned the classroom. She appreciated the silent respect offered by the other students, then looked again at Mina and continued softly, "Mina, if you have a few minutes after class, I can help you."

Mina stood with her mouth open. It was the first nice thing this professor had said to her since school began.

"Thank you, Professor Abbar! I will stay. I will," she stammered. "And . . . thank you!"

Rafia smiled at Mina. "It's no problem. I'm glad to help you."

Fifteen minutes later, Mina and her professor sat alone in the classroom, and again, the instructor's words were pleasantly surprising.

"Mina, you have great possibilities as a student. I've been hard on you this year, and your discouragement shows, but please know that I am taking you on as a personal challenge." Rafia folded her hands in her lap and faced Mina. "I'm willing to work with you for the rest of the school year." She patted her own chest with her right hand. "Believe it or not, I was a lot like you. I did not start working hard until my second year in college." Rafia paused and shook her head. "But with your grades, you cannot afford to wait that long!"

"I'm shocked, professor. I thought you disliked me, but I do thank you." Mina looked at the floor, then back at Rafia before continuing. "Would you consider working with me for the rest of my years in college?"

Rafia nodded. "I would, Mina, but after this year, I'm off to Australia. I've been given a grant to earn another master's degree in women's studies at the University of Sydney. I'll be gone for a year."

"That sounds wonderful—and also like quite an honor."

"Yes. Thank you, Mina. It is a very special opportunity. My husband even thinks I should take our daughter with me. She and I are very close, and I'm afraid my little Noureen couldn't bear having me gone so long. I would also miss her terribly, of course." Rafia patted both knees with her hands and stood up. "So, Mina, we have a few months to work together to teach *you* how to memorize more effectively—and more important, how to live for Allah as a committed Muslim woman. Are you ready to give it your best?"

Mina stood quickly. "I am!"

Six months later, Rafia and Noureen Abbar boarded a plane at Riyadh's King Khalid International Airport and readied themselves for the fifteen-hour flight to Sydney. Their seatmate had already settled by the window.

"I'm Emma." The non-Arab woman smiled. "What's your name?"

"I'm Rafia. Rafia Abbar, and this is my daughter, Noureen."

"Noureen, how old are you?"

The girl looked up at her mother. "She's ten," Rafia said on behalf of her daughter.

"You're both from Saudi Arabia? I noticed your beautiful head coverings and thought you might be from here."

"Yes. That's right. We're Saudis." Rafia guessed this chatty female was an American.

"All I've gotten to do is change planes here at the airport. I've always wanted to really visit Saudi Arabia, though. I just love the Middle East."

Rafia nodded as she helped Noureen buckle her seatbelt.

"I think most Muslims are misunderstood—by other people, I mean. You know: CNN, Fox News, and all that." Rafia startled as Emma placed a hand on Rafia's left arm. "I've prayed for the Islamic people for years now."

Rafia cocked her head and eyed the talkative woman. "Why have you prayed for us?"

For several seconds, Emma seemed to measure Rafia's question, and then answered. "Well, since you asked . . . I think God is after Muslims, frankly. He is honoring them. I've been hearing a lot about Muslims having dreams about Jesus. And they're not the kind of dreams someone has after a bad plate of baba ghanoush or something like that. These are high-definition dreams—visions!—of Jesus, and good-hearted Muslims who have them end up asking Jesus followers what they mean. Isn't that cool?"

Rafia felt her pulse quicken but simply nodded as the flight crew's safety instructions cut short the conversation.

Noureen had fallen asleep ten minutes after takeoff, and for several more minutes, Emma had noticed Rafia staring at the back of the seat in front of her. Suddenly, she turned to Emma.

"I've been having dreams about Jesus."

Emma's eyes widened.

"For about six months now."

Emma said nothing to Rafia but prayed silently that the Holy Spirit would give her the right words to say. Just before the silence became awkward, she replied, "This is no accident, Rafia—you and I meeting here on this plane, I mean. The Lord Jesus wants you to know, more than anything, how much He loves you."

"We believe in Jesus—or *Isa*, as the Quran calls Him. He's a great prophet. I understand that."

"Rafia, Jesus was a prophet, and He was also a priest. But you may not realize He was much more than that. May I tell you about Him? He also is King."

A year later, Rafia and Noureen boarded the Emirates Triple-7 morning flight from Sydney to Riyadh, her master's of women's studies now solidly part of her curriculum vitae. Both Abbars were excited to see in person family members they had seen only on Skype during the past twelve months. And both mother and daughter now shared a common love for Jesus.

Rafia leaned back in her seat and marveled at her life. *A professor of sharia law is now a follower of Jesus. What will this bring? I live in one of the most dangerous places in the world to become a believer in Christ.* Rafia was concerned, but she smiled as she recalled the flight that had started the remarkable, year-long journey she and Noureen had just spent in Australia.

That day a year back, after Rafia Abbar had told Emma Rylee about her dreams of Jesus, the two women had talked for nearly fifteen hours straight en route to Sydney. Emma's faith was vibrantly real, and her passion "for religion" was something Rafia had never seen in anyone—even the imams. One by one, Rafia had told Emma about each of her five nighttime encounters with Jesus, and in Emma, the professor from Riyadh finally found someone who could answer the long list of questions the dreams had inspired.

Rafia had easily believed Emma's assertion that God had brought the two women together. Emma was traveling to Sydney to begin school at the University of Sydney. The two would be fellow students!

Once in Australia, Rafia's dreams had continued, and as Emma had suggested, Rafia, hungry to know the truth about this Jesus, had started reading the Scriptures. Professor Abbar had read the entire New Testament and simply couldn't stop. She had read it again. And then again.

Rafia remembered one particular morning when she had been reading Matthew 16, where Peter proclaimed that Jesus was *the Messiah*. But it was what Jesus said next that shook Rafia to the core: "What good will it be for someone to gain the whole world, yet forfeit his soul? Or what can anyone give in exchange for his soul?" (Matt. 16:26).

At that moment, Islam and Christianity had fallen into sharp relief. Muslims, she realized, are taught that you can never be sure if you will go to heaven or not. Even Muhammad did not know his fate. Yet Rafia had wanted to know hers. She desperately did not want to lose her soul for all eternity.

That was the morning Emma had called right after Rafia's reading of the Matthew passage. She had invited the Muslim professor to church. It was a frightening prospect but also irresistible. She had prayed with Noureen before leaving for the meeting with Emma.

"Okay, Jesus, I know You are more than a prophet, but please give me a sign. You told us 'to ask and you will receive.' So I'm asking, Jesus. I want to believe. Show us how."

Rafia had barely set foot in the door of the meeting room when two women in Muslim head coverings rushed to hug her. "*Habibti!*"* they had shouted.

*Other Muslims like me are here to study the Bible? Not only that, these two are Arabs—from Saudi Arabia!* Their greeting

---

* An affectionate greeting between Muslim women

had dashed Rafia's hope of entering the gathering unnoticed, and that night, when a young man stood to read the Scripture the group was to study, the words had stunned her: "What good will it be for someone to gain the whole world, yet forfeit his soul? Or what can anyone give in exchange for his soul?"

Rafia had asked Jesus for a sign, and He had given her two. The Muslim women were not only from Saudi Arabia, but lived in Riyadh. Then Jeremy, the group leader, had read the same scripture she had struggled with that morning. Jesus' words had tugged at her heart. She did not doubt that nothing in this life could compare in importance to eternity. Suddenly she had also realized there was only one way to face it, and that is with Jesus.

Mother and daughter had both given their lives to Jesus that day. And now, on their way back to Saudi Arabia, they knew it meant they had truly given Him everything. Before boarding the plane, her two fellow believers from Riyadh had prayed for the return trip, and Samia had concluded with a bold affirmation: "Lord, we know You have called us to be ready to die for You. Rafia goes back to her home now, and we do not know what awaits her. In Saudi Arabia, we are like the Thessalonians, who welcomed the message of Jesus in the midst of intense suffering."

Rafia and Noureen settled in for the long flight to the Kingdom of Saudi Arabia. As the wheels lifted off the runway, Rafia opened her Bible and turned to 1 Thessalonians 1:4 and read, "For we know, brothers and sisters loved by God, that he has chosen you."

Rafia's mind drifted. *Do I tell my family immediately? Do I tell Ismail? He is not a deeply committed Muslim, but I could see this being the spark that lights a fire in him for Islam.* She looked out the window at the ground shrinking below the airplane. *I must get stronger.* She promised herself that she would go as soon as possible to the underground church Samia and Jala had told her about. *I must be ready before I tell my family. I could die.*

Rafia reached for her daughter and stroked the little girl's soft, black hair. "Nouri, let's not tell anyone about Jesus right away. We can make it a surprise for them when the time is right. Okay, my precious love?"

"Okay, Mommy." Noureen pressed her head against her mother's hand.


One week later, Professor Abbar skipped lunch and slipped, unnoticed, into a house just off campus. A meeting referred to simply as the Way was to start at noon.

"Professor Abbar?"

Rafia startled at hearing her name and turned around to face the voice. In the last year, Rafia's life had seen one surprise after another, but nothing had prepared her for this one.

"It's me: Mina. Do you remember me?"

This time, Rafia's jaw dropped. "Do I remember you? Of course! Mina, what are you doing here?"

"Well, I guess I could ask you the same question, Professor Abbar."

The woman reached for her former student. "Mina, are you here because . . ."

"Because I love Jesus? Yes. I am!" Mina grabbed the professor's outstretched hands. "That is the *very* reason I'm here." The two women hugged. "While you were gone, my interest in religion just fizzled. But I met some people from the Way, and . . ." Mina looked Rafia in the eye. "Have you heard about Muslims having dreams of Jesus?"

"Well, yes, I have." Rafia smiled.

Mina glanced across the room and back at her older friend. "They're getting started, Professor. Can we sit together?"

"That would be delightful. But in these meetings, Mina, I'm just Rafia. Please, call me Rafia."

"It's a deal."

The two women picked their way through the thirty people assembled in the room and found an open space to sit down. To Rafia's surprise, Mina stood back up and addressed the group.

"I have to speak about something." Mina had found her public voice and impressed Rafia with her presence in front of the gathering. "My father has become a fundamentalist Muslim. He practiced Islam, but everything changed when his brother went to work for the secret police. He's a different man now.

"He has also been asking me questions lately." She chuckled. "He says I look different, and he's right, of course. The Holy Spirit lives inside of me!"

The room exploded in applause.

Mina motioned for quiet. "Unfortunately, he is suspicious. So, before I say anything else, I must tell you that if my phone rings and it's my father, I will run out of here as fast as I can and take the call outside. If he found me reading the Bible and worshipping Jesus, he would not give it a second thought. He would kill me. In fact, he would have every one of us killed right here, right now, if he knew."

Mina took a deep breath and looked around the room. "We are the new church at Thessalonica, and Jesus has called us to suffer for Him."

The meeting closed in prayer at exactly one o'clock. Students and the few professors in attendance exited quickly.

As Rafia and Mina strolled up the sidewalk together toward campus, Mina spoke more seriously than she had at the meeting. "Rafia, when I go home each day, my father interrogates me. He asks me questions about the Quran. I've even seen him peek into my religion class to check on me, but I pretend I don't see him.

"I admit that sometimes I battle discouragement. How oppressive it is to live like this, under a microscope! But how I thank Jesus for the Way! Oh, Rafia, I love the simple faith we have, reading Jesus' words and then challenging each other to live this truth." She took her friend's arm. "I need the accountability to make sure I'm faithful to what He has called us to do."

Rafia nodded and listened quietly.

"I love following Jesus, Rafia. My life was so empty. I thought I was free on my trips to Dubai, but that life was bankrupt. Partying is such a dead-end street! I'm ashamed of how I lived before Jesus gave me real freedom. Forgiveness is the true liberation!"

Rafia nodded again, and the two women walked for half a block in silence.

As they reached the corner where they would part, Mina stopped and looked firmly at the professor. "I'm not afraid, Rafia. Are you?"

"Not really."

Mina nodded. "Have a great weekend."


Rafia decided to make the Way a secret part of her schedule. She would try to attend all three meetings each week. The following Monday at noon, the Way gathered, and several more bodies wedged into the floor space. Rafia noticed immediately that Mina was not in the room.

Kareem opened the meeting with an announcement, his tone serious. "Since Friday, we have lost contact with Mina. I've called several times, and her phone goes straight to voice mail. Several of us have talked, and we fear her uncle may have taken her—or worse."

The announcement distracted Rafia for the rest of the meeting. Absorbed in her own thoughts, she could not focus on the Bible study. By the closing prayer, though, Rafia had made a decision, and that night at the family dinner table, she made an announcement of her own.

An uncle and his family had joined Ismail, Noureen, and Rafia. As she finished the last of her food, Rafia stood up and cleared her throat. Calmly, she looked at each of her family members in turn, then spoke succinctly. "I love Jesus, and I follow *Him* now. I'm not practicing Islam anymore."

Eyes that had been focused on Rafia quickly looked down at their dinner plates. Rafia sat down. Silence amplified the shuffle of her chair. No one made eye contact with anyone else. Not even Ismail looked at his wife. Only Noureen looked at her mother. She smiled.

For the next two days, everyone ignored the awkward meal. Ismail barely noticed his wife. The night of the dinner, though, one simple, unheard-of act by her husband had made Rafia's flesh crawl. Without a word at bedtime, he had picked up his pillow from the bed, walked down the hall into the guest room, and closed the door. Both nights since, Ismail had said nothing to Rafia but had slept in a separate room. Rafia realized the only thing normal about Ismail was that he still tickled Noureen each time she walked by, but he picked their daughter up more often than usual, hugging her warmly.

On the third night, Rafia decided to call her young friend one more time.

"Hi. This is Mina. Leave me a message," was the only reply.

The next day at the Way, the group was somber. Kareem confirmed that Mina was dead. An uncle had beaten her to death.

The thought of her vibrant young friend's death sickened Rafia. She muddled through afternoon classes, hoping her students wouldn't notice how distant she was. When the eternal afternoon finally ended, Rafia retreated home. Ismail had said he would be working late, so she and Noureen would have the house to themselves. The torment of Mina's death exhausted Rafia, and as soon as she had tucked Noureen in for the night, she fell into her own bed and welcomed sleep.

A few minutes after midnight, Rafia drifted into semiconsciousness. Jesus had never quoted the Quran in one of her dreams, yet she was not sure that she was dreaming.

No! She really *was* hearing a male voice reciting Koranic Suras.

She opened her eyes and gasped. In the dim light from the lamp in the hallway—she could only guess that Ismail must have turned it on when he came home—she could see the blade of a knife suspended inches from her face. The voice concluded a sura. She recognized the verse and realized it was a judgment pronounced over her, and a second knife suddenly wavered next to the first.

"Rafia. How could you?"

Beyond the daggers, Rafia discerned the faces of two uncles. Perhaps Ismail had not been working late but had chosen to stay away from *this* business. The male relatives were no doubt here to restore the family honor.

"I love You, Jesus," Rafia whispered. "Into Your hands, I commit my spirit."

Rafia Abbar did not resist. She felt peace and closed her eyes.

Several seconds passed, and she wondered why she had not yet felt the slash of knife blades into her flesh. After several more seconds, she opened her eyes and saw the knives quivering in front of her. She squinted past the blades and puzzled over the distress on her executioners' faces. For ten full minutes, they stood frozen above her, knives in hand. Then, as if obeying orders, the two men sheathed the weapons and bustled out the bedroom door.

Rafia turned to watch them leave and was horrified to see Noureen just inside the room, leaning against the wall, watching.

"Oh, sweetie! Mommy is so sorry you had to see this!" Rafia plunged to her knees beside the bed and bear-hugged her daughter. "We must go. Now! We will grab a few things we will need and leave." She looked the little girl in the eye. "Do you understand? We are not safe, Nouri."

The girl nodded, strangely unperturbed. "Mommy, I knew Grandpa's brothers would not kill you."

Rafia raised an eyebrow. "Honey, how did you know that? Why do you say that?"

Noureen grinned. "Didn't you see Jesus standing in front of you? *He* was holding their arms back. They didn't hurt you because they couldn't. Jesus was there, Mommy. He wouldn't let them touch you."

## A MESSAGE FROM RAFIA

I never saw Jesus standing over me, protecting me. I was ready to die.

Nouri told me later that while my uncles held the knives in my face, Jesus looked at her, and He smiled. Standing strong in His white robe, He was in control. His smile told Noureen that Mommy was not in danger. O, my loving Savior—my heavenly Bodyguard!

But I have had to ask the question: "Why am I here, yet Mina was taken?"

Looking back over her dear life, I see how the Lord brought us together. Until we met Jesus, I didn't realize we had both struggled with emptiness. She had tried to fill hers with wild parties, while I tried with strict religion. We'd both wanted peace, and we both had come up empty.

Still, it troubles me that Mina was so young when her life was taken. Even when her questions and lack of preparation for class made me angry, I could not help but love that girl. Her enthusiasm for living was contagious. Now, at twenty years old, she is a martyr for Jesus. It was her great privilege to die for Him, and I am honored to have known her for even a short time.

So why am I alive, and Mina is with Jesus? The answer is that she and I are *both* alive. In fact, she is more alive now than ever! This is the great lesson I've learned from thinking about her death—and the deaths of any martyrs. Too often, even Christians forget that our faith is not primarily for this life. It is for the life to come. We who are still here are the ones who have been left behind. Our real life has not even begun, but for martyrs like Mina, it has.

When you live in Saudi Arabia and give yourself to Jesus, you forfeit your right to live. The cost is known from the beginning. But Jesus assured all of us that whoever loses his life for His sake will save it (Matt. 16:25). Paul also told the Thessalonians not to be "unsettled by these trials. For you know quite well that we are destined for them" (1 Thess. 3:3).

The trials we endure reinforce our identity in Christ. They offer evidence that we are no longer children of the devil but are children in the family of God.

I have, of course, resigned from the university. I was in anguish over the prospect of following Jesus. After all, I was a professor in a respected Islamic university and a teacher of sharia law, but how could I go on teaching *that?* Yet how could I leave the religion I had so faithfully studied and taught with passion all these years?

Ultimately, the answer is simple. I followed Jesus because He is the only one who could fill my empty soul. I may have been a religious zealot, but I ached to know God and could not find Him even though I had searched all my life. Meeting Emma Rylee began to adjust my thinking. She had a joy that I completely lacked. I could feel it just being around her, and I wanted the same—very badly.

As for my family, they all now know about the miracle of protection from my uncles. No one has spoken openly about it, though. I remain apart from them—Nouri and I moved across town—but I am sure someday they will try to avenge the family honor again. I remain a blight on all of them. But until they kill me, I try to live as Jesus would by serving them and letting them see the grace and love of God in me.

Mina was privileged to be with Jesus before me, but I believe I will be there soon. Meanwhile, I am His servant in Saudi Arabia. And by the way, so is my sweet one, little Nouri. Together, we are memorizing Paul's letters to the Thessalonians.

Please pray for your family in Saudi Arabia.

# CHAPTER SEVEN

# WHEN THE BROTHERHOOD HAS A KNIFE AT YOUR THROAT

SAMER ISMAIL SCRAMBLED onto the empty main stage and gasped as he stood up to view the horde. *So this is what a million people gathered in one place looks like.* From the southwest quadrant of Tahrir Square, he also thought it appeared that all of Egypt must be assembled here in Cairo today.

Al Jazeera claimed this to be one of the largest gatherings in modern history, and Samer and his best friend, Yousef, were firsthand witnesses to this world-changing event! The crowd had expanded by the hour, and now it overflowed onto every side street, rooftop, and balcony adjacent to the square.

"Can you believe we're actually here?" Samer yelled toward Yousef. His friend had joined him, and they stood with their shoulders nearly touching. Yet Yousef still strained to hear Samer over the bedlam of the crowd.

A million Egyptians smelled blood, and President Hosni Mubarak was the one bleeding. After enduring thirty years of his ruthless regime, the masses had found their voice, and the world seemed to be listening.

When protests had first started, two weeks earlier, the "revolution" in Tahrir Square had looked more like a rerun of typical Egyptian political demonstrations. The people assemble, the crowds swell, the army arrives and shoots a few key protestors, and then the gathering breaks up. But this was different. After an initially tough response, the army appeared indecisive. Samer had friends in the military, and he had heard rumors that all were not unquestionably loyal to the president.

Samer pointed to a line of military police stretched between the crowds and four tanks along the eastern curve of the traffic circle where Talaat Harb exits the square. "They're going to defect! I can feel it! I saw it in their eyes when we were over there earlier today. They're sympathetic! How can they *not* hate all the corruption?"

Yousef merely nodded and jabbed his friend's shoulder with his fist.

The front-end brutality of Mubarak's military had been seen instantly around the globe on Facebook and Twitter. A new generation and a new revolution went viral on new technology from Cairo. Every dictator who ever lived was being reviled.

In an odd pairing of cultures, Che Guevara became the icon around which protestors rallied. The throwback Cuban revolutionary of the 1950s appeared on T-shirts by the thousand in

Tahrir Square. He was the poster boy for Egyptian resistance to the Mubarak regime, but apparently the mobs had forgotten the results of Cuba's "liberation" under Castro. As too often happens in revolutions, idealism mixed with youth creates the perfect power vacuum—and lays out the welcome mat for budding dictators. Even now, several would-be tyrants waited for events to unfold in Egypt, and each had one thing in common: they were members of the Muslim Brotherhood.

"This is what we've waited for our whole lives!" Palms stretched toward the tumult, Samer thrust his arms in the air. He joined a thousand other dissidents whose emotions cast aside reason as if it were irrelevant to the moment.

"Mubarak must go! We will not be silenced!" Yousef raised his arms and joined Samer in chanting with the crowd assembled near the stage.

The sun began to set on the noisy mass, and as darkness seeped into Tahrir Square, orators replaced Samer and Yousef on the platform. Protest choruses ebbed and flowed well into the night.

Twelve hours after they had joined the protests, Samer and Yousef walked several blocks to the Qasr al-Nil Bridge and crossed over the Nile River to open areas on the opposite bank. The thrum of the crowd a half mile away continued as the two young men stretched out their sleeping bags on the grass and lay down.

"Yousef, did you hear about the thirteen-year-old boy from my city that our dear president had the police torture a few months ago?"

Yousef Mansour rolled over on his sleeping bag, anxious to hear the whole story.

"It was punishment because the boy stole a bag of tea! The police beat and *raped* him, then left him for dead by some railroad tracks."

Yousef grimaced.

"I sometimes think Mubarak treats you Christians better than he does us Muslims."

"I see what you mean, Samer, but I think his hatred has no religious preference. Last year, word on the street was that in Al-Minya the fundamentalists planned to burn down several Coptic churches. We called the police, told them about the rumor, and they promised to be on standby for an immediate response if we called for help." Yousef huffed. "They were true to their word. They stood by. Yes, they did—until every last church was a pile of ashes. *Then* they showed up."

Yousef propped himself on an elbow and continued. "Samer, you're a Muslim, and I'm a Christian. You were born in a small village, and I was born in Alexandria. When we met at Cairo University, we could not have been more different. But we get along fine. And you know why that is?"

Samer nodded. The two of them had covered this ground before.

"It's because we are *Egyptians!* Both of us are proud of our heritage. This is the country where Muslims and Christians can live side by side with no problem. And when we overthrow Mr. Mubarak, we will be an example of peaceful coexistence to the world!"

"You can bet on that one, my friend!" Samer raised a clenched hand, and the two friends did a fist pump and punch, then flopped onto their backs, chuckling at their routine.

As they lay a few dozen feet from the slow-moving waters of the Nile, the distant crowd was the only sound between the two. After several minutes, Samer whispered to his college roommate.

"Yousef, one last thing: I think you're rubbing off on me." Samer stared at the sky. "I've been having some interesting dreams lately . . . *Jesus* is in them. We must talk." He cocked his head toward Yousef and laughed quietly. "But I guess it won't be tonight."

Yousef was sound asleep.


Omar Makram Mosque in Tahrir Square blasted the morning call to prayer and jarred the two friends awake. Cairo's legion of mosques followed suit, and the *adhan* echoed in all directions.

Samer rose to his knees and stretched his prayer rug on the grass beside him. Yousef took out his Bible and closed his eyes to pray before reading. As Samer repeated his prayers, he peeked at Yousef until the friend opened his eyes and began reading the holy book. Samer finished his ritual, sat back on the prayer rug, and looked across the river toward the square and its mosque.

The Omar Makram was named in honor of an Egyptian hero who led the resistance against Napoleon's invasion in 1798.

*Our symbol in the age-old fight against tyranny,* thought Samer. He smiled. Today the call from the mosque had seemed louder than usual, beckoning the multitude to another day of demonstrations for freedom.

"The world will see us today," Samer whispered to himself, thinking about the expanding global news coverage of the events in Tahrir Square. He turned and saw that Yousef had closed his Bible and set it on his sleeping bag.

"Yousef, if you could kill Mubarak, would you do it?" Samer blurted out the question louder than he had intended.

Yousef smirked at his friend's abrupt foray into political topics. He shook his head. "I couldn't go that far, Samer. I'm praying for a peaceful end to this. Besides, today is Egypt's Day of Love in Tahrir Square. We can't think about killing. People are in this together. Did you see the chain of protection formed by a group of Christians around Muslims as they prayed at noon yesterday? It was a beautiful thing to watch everyone pull together as Egyptians."

"Well, Yousef, whatever they call today, I'm just glad the water cannons and the tear gas are gone. The government now knows that kind of crowd control doesn't work when you have over a million protestors." Samer gazed across the water and smiled.

"I think the most bizarre day of this ordeal was last week." Yousef rummaged in his backpack for morning food. "When the troops stormed on camels through the protestors, I knew how desperate Mubarak was! Man, that whip left a hefty stripe on my back!"

"And I can still feel the knot on my head from the rod that hit me." Samer reached for the labneh* and cucumber pita sandwich Yousef held out to him. "I'm just glad we avoided the camel riders with *swords*."

"This has been a journey, hasn't it? A Muslim and his best friend—a Christian—survived Tahrir Square. Sounds like a movie script to me."

Samer chuckled as he bit into breakfast.

"Our journey may soon be over, too. With the army no longer fighting us, how much more can this last?"

Samer swallowed and added his own commentary. "One thing would turn the protest into a celebration: if President Mubarak resigned, the world would be invited to an Egyptian party that hasn't been seen since the time of Pharaoh!"

The day of their dreams was approaching more quickly than either Yousef or Samer imagined, but first they would have to survive yet another stint in Tahrir Square—the Day of Love.

"Tear off her clothes!"

Over the next fourteen hours, Samer and Yousef witnessed a crowd filled with anything but love. By ten o'clock that night, when failed generators plunged the square into darkness, protestors degenerated still further into a frenzy of heinous acts.

The thirty-three-year-old woman screamed as a group of men threw her to the ground. Fifteen pairs of hands grappled for

_____

* Strained yogurt

her clothing, stripped her naked, and held her to the pavement as each in turn raped the sobbing female. In a chain reaction, male protestors formed other groups, and, to shouts of *"Allahu Akbar!"*[*] ripped the clothing off of any woman in proximity. In seconds, more than a dozen women lay helpless and naked under feverish men.

Recovering from their initial shock and disbelief at what was happening around them, Samer and Yousef jumped onto a pile of attackers and grabbed hair, clothing, and arms to pull them away from the gang rape of a sixteen-year-old girl. They wrenched one molester after another out of the heap until they reached the bottom and the unconscious victim. Samer and Yousef pulled off their shirts to cover the motionless teen and scooped her off the ground.

As the two friends carried Laila Amir away from the crowd and toward the Nile River, police arrived and began beating the rapists with nightsticks. Several Muslim women caught up with Samer and Yousef and threw shawls over the girl as police continued to fight back the mob.

Three hours later, Samer and Yousef, still in shock, hung their heads over the sides of the Qasr al-Nil Bridge. Exhausted from the exertion of extricating the young woman from her attackers and from multiple rounds of questions they answered for a crime report at the police station after seeing the girl to a hospital, neither could find the words to express all they were feeling at the moment. As if the assembly in Tahrir Square was

---

* Allah is greatest!"

itself stunned at the events of the past several hours, noise from the scene seemed more subdued than the previous night.

Samer was the first to express his heartbreak. "Yousef, they were yelling 'Allahu Akbar'! What could be more perverted?" He squeezed his eyes shut, and Yousef suspected his friend was working hard to hold back tears. "That girl—she was helpless. She was there like us—to rejoice in the victory of the people! How could they?!" He turned toward Yousef. "Look at my face! I was beaten to a pulp trying to help. So were you! They were animals! You and I were lucky to make it out alive. And she was, too!"

Samer stared downriver as moonlight sparkled on the water, then continued solemnly. "Muslim men molesting a young Muslim girl. I wonder what she thinks of our religion now? I hope those beasts get a life sentence. Theirs is *not* the religion my father taught me."

"I know that, Samer." Yousef's gaze paralleled his friend's. "I've never seen anything so horrible. This is one of the saddest days of my life. I can hardly imagine how things got so vile so fast. The demons of hell must have been released to do their work as soon as the lights went out." He glanced at the sky and said, mostly to himself, "The whole world lies in the power of the evil one."

The two men stared at the river in silence for several minutes before Samer spoke again. "Yousef, do you know what you did? You risked your life for a Muslim girl. I could imagine that you would do that for a Christian, but . . ."

"I don't think that way, Samer. I don't see *religion* when I look at a person. Tonight I risked my life for another human being. That girl . . . Laila . . . was created in the image of God. All of us are. If she had been a Christian, I believe you would have been right there with me, trying to rescue her." Yousef looked up again and said softly, "I pray that she lives."

Samer broke down but tried to hide his sobs from Yousef.

"Come on, Samer." Yousef tapped his friend on the shoulder. "Let's go get some sleep."

The two companions headed toward the grassy area where they had slept the night before. Suddenly, Yousef grinned. "By the way, did you learn those moves watching cage fighting on TV?" He slapped his buddy on the biceps. "Man, you've got a future."

Samer forced a smile. "You weren't too bad yourself, Yousef."

"After weeks of protest in Cairo and other cities of Egypt," the voice of Vice President Omar Suleiman boomed from the sound system into a Tahrir Square awash in light from the now-working generators, "Hosni Mubarak has stepped down as president of Egypt!"

Hundreds of thousands of protestors erupted in cheers.

Suleiman continued over the pandemonium, "In the name of God the merciful, the compassionate: citizens, during these very difficult circumstances Egypt is going through, President Hosni Mubarak has decided to step down from the office of president of the republic and has charged the high council of the armed forces to administer the affairs of the country. May God help everybody!"

The horrifying events of the Day of Love forgotten in the tumult of the moment, Samer and Yousef hugged each other and wept. Thirty years of Hosni Mubarak's reign were over! And after only eighteen days of protesting! A new name for Tahrir Square rippled through the crowd: *Liberation* Square!

Swarms of people chanted:

"Egypt is Free! Egypt is free!"

"Hold your heads high, Egyptians!"

"The crescent and the cross together!"

Fireworks exploded overhead, and the mass roared anew as Egyptian Air Force planes screamed across the sky. Even while they shouted, thousands held hands over their ears against the overwhelming decibels.

Many stood in shock, looking like statues of Pharaoh in the Cairo Museum. Strangers hugged strangers. Parents tossed giggling children in the air. Some merely bowed low and kissed the ground.

*"Bilady, Bilady, Bilady"*\* blared over loudspeakers. Young people waved Egyptian flags from atop parked army tanks. Yousef and Samer reveled in the Tahrir Square party, making easy friends everywhere they surfed the crowd, but by four in the morning, they had had enough and plodded across the bridge to their hangout by the river. Thousands of people still sat up on the lawns and reviewed with one another the day's historic events.

"Yousef, my friend!" Samer stood on his sleeping bag and

---

\*The Egyptian national anthem: "My Homeland, My Homeland, My Homeland."

raised his arms. "We go to sleep tonight as *free men!* For the first time in our lives, this is our reality!"

The two friends offered each other one last fist pump and flopped onto the ground, exhilarated and exhausted. Sleep came before either had time to consider what the events they had witnessed in the previous few days might portend for this "new Egypt." And neither anticipated Who would visit with Samer later that night.

*"Samer!"* The white-robed Man in the dream spoke firmly but kindly. *"If the Son sets you free, you will be free indeed."*

Two and a half years later, in summer 2013, Samer and Yousef met again in Cairo. As expected, life in Egypt had changed—but not in the ways they had hoped. Even so, the cloud had a silver lining: one of the two was a radically changed person.

"Well, Yousef, my friend, here we are, back in Tahrir Square. Kind of like being home, isn't it?"

"In a strange sort of way, yes. You're a different man than you were before, though. And may I say that I'm thankful—for your sake?!"

Samer grinned.

"You're a new creation—and now my brother in Christ, Samer! How cool is that! And what a contrast our new mission is from last time." Yousef swept a hand toward the crowd—perhaps even larger than the victory gathering of two years earlier.

"Yes, it is! Once I saw the Light, I could not walk away from it." Samer chuckled. "Did you know I used to sneak your Bible sometimes when you were asleep, and read it? I even did it on a few of those nights when we camped by the Nile during the revolution." Samer paused before continuing, his tone subdued. "I haven't told my family about my new faith. Some of my friends know, and hopefully they won't tell my parents. I have relatives who are quite fanatical, and now that the Muslim Brotherhood is in power, *they* feel empowered."

"Samer, your relatives must be horrified now that Egypt has turned against Mohamed Morsi. Just a year ago, the Brotherhood leadership went from life in prison to running the country. And now it's all turned back on them. Look at this crowd today. Just like before, Christians and Muslims are standing shoulder to shoulder. Yet the church in Egypt has been under siege this year. Churches have been routinely burned to the ground."

Samer interrupted, incensed. "Yes. And in my village near Asyut, more than seventy girls were kidnapped and held for ransom. Kidnappings happen every week. And, Yousef, the rapes we witnessed in Tahrir Square during this 'great revolution' have become commonplace. What is wrong with our people?

"I tell you," Samer continued, growing angrier. "As a country, we could not bear this weight anymore. We need relief from the madness of the Muslim Brotherhood's tyranny. Women and girls were not safe. Neither were Coptic Christians or Muslims who didn't support sharia law. We need more change!"

Yousef nodded. "Samer, can you believe how many Muslims have become followers of Jesus?"

"Absolutely! It's ironic. I wanted a revolution for Egypt, but all the time Jesus was pursuing me for my own revolution! I know that's happened to others, too." Samer pointed toward the main stage, assembled on the same spot as during the 2011 demonstrations. "Today I want nothing more than to stand on that platform and tell all my Muslim friends what has happened to me!"

"Samer, I appreciate your excitement, but Christians and Muslims aren't getting along *that* well here. We both might get killed if you try it." Yousef cocked his head toward his friend and scowled light-heartedly.

"Then how about we do what Jesus told His disciples to do when He sent them out in Luke 10? Let's fast today and prayer-walk around Liberation Square, and up and down the Nile River. That's all we'll do for the whole day. I've learned something these past two years: less doing and more praying!"

"All right. Then tomorrow let's also come back here and pray that Jesus leads us to a person of peace. He promised that the 'harvest is plentiful.'" Yousef clasped his hands together. "And today, Lord Jesus, we pray that a harvest of souls will turn to You in the capital city of Egypt."

Samer nodded at Yousef's prayer. "Just think about it, bro. Jesus has called us to spread His message in the spiritual headquarters of Sunni Islam! You know what they say: 'As Cairo goes, so goes the Arab Muslim world.' How honored we are to pray here and share Jesus' love in the midst of Egypt's continuing turmoil."

Samer's voice trailed off as he looked toward the Omar

Makram Mosque. For nearly a minute, he pondered the scene before speaking again.

"Yousef, I've been watching that group over there at the mosque. You see them on the edge of the square?"

Yousef nodded.

"They're vicious. They see Egypt rejecting *their* beloved leader so quickly that it's made them very, very angry." He raised his left hand to his chin. "Look at their signs screaming hatred for everyone who opposes them.

"Last night they were burning Bibles again too. How sick that they urinate on God's Word and then light them on fire. Can you imagine what would happen if someone did that to a Quran?"

He turned to Yousef. "Did you know that the Tamarod opposition group has already gotten 22 *million* signatures calling for early elections to replace President Morsi? The news says this may be the largest protest in human history. Every major city square in Egypt is packed with people. I know my family in Alexandria says they've never witnessed such a phenomenon—and you know how strong the Brotherhood is in Lower Egypt." He paused again before concluding, "All eyes are on us."

"The great Muslim Brotherhood dream of ruling Egypt and spreading across the Arab world is about to come to an end," Yousef added softly.

"If my family knew about my conversion . . ." Samer's voice trailed off.

Yousef placed a hand on his friend's right shoulder. "Yeah,

Samer, they're a scary mob. Evil oozes out of them, but I pray: Lord Jesus, reveal Yourself to them!"

Yousef patted Samer's shoulder, then pointed at Tahrir Square. "Let's start walking and praying, in different directions. The Cairo Museum will be our rendezvous point." Yousef pointed over his shoulder at the building behind them. "And by the way, did you hear that General al-Sisi has been visiting hospitals in Cairo to apologize to rape victims and their families? I wish *he* were leading our country."

Samer shook his head. "Then he must've spent a whole week at the hospital seeing the victims. There were forty-six rapes in Tahrir Square in just the last few months. The Lord only knows how many more went unreported." He sneered in disgust.

"Okay, my friend, let's brighten up. We're here for Kingdom work this time. How about I walk west and you walk east? We'll meet back here in front of the museum at 3:00 p.m."

Heat from the Saharan sun matched the rage of the Muslim Brotherhood gathered in Tahrir Square. On this last day of June 2013, protestors sensed that Mohamed Morsi was about to be forcibly removed from office by the Egyptian military, led by General al-Sisi. Mimicking the call for penalty in a soccer game, protestors waved red cards all across the open space. Members of the Brotherhood dove into the sea of red, intent on adding the crimson of blood. Rape gangs and men with knives swarmed into the masses and added violence to the chaos.

At three o'clock in the afternoon, Yousef pushed his way through the madness toward the Cairo Museum to wait for Samer. At four o'clock, he was still waiting.

Yousef Mansour never saw his best friend again. An hour after sunset, he trudged across the Qasr al-Nil Bridge and passed a nearly sleepless night on the grass, fearing the worst for his one-time college roommate.

At daybreak, Yousef's cell phone woke him.

"Yousef, this is Michael. I'm in Cairo."

Yousef had not realized his cousin, too, was in town. "Michael, are you all right?"

"Yes. But I have news of Samer. He is *not* all right." The voice paused. "Samer had stopped to pray by the mosque when the Brotherhood took him. He had been reading the Bible to a young Morsi supporter who seemed interested, and he wouldn't leave, even when the shooting started between the army and the Brotherhood. A group of clerics saw what he was doing and dragged him away."

Michael paused again, then said, "Yousef, Samer is dead."

Without a word, Yousef clicked off the phone and slipped it into his pocket. He stood paralyzed, staring across the Nile River in the direction of Omar Makram Mosque and the horde of people, which included the murderers of his best friend. A thought played in his mind. *Samer was martyred in Tahrir Square. Samer was martyred in Tahrir Square. Samer was martyred in . . . Martyr's Square.*

Six months later, Yousef still thought of his best friend almost daily. Crowds had faded from city squares all over the country, but home in Alexandria, Yousef faced serious trouble.

The now-deposed Muslim Brotherhood had launched a killing spree targeting pastors. One by one, church leaders—including some of Yousef's friends—were given the "opportunity" to make a decision: *convert to Islam or die.*

Yousef sipped the last of his second cup of coffee and looked his longtime friend Pastor Said in the eye. "Where are the police these days? Is ignoring us their new standard operating procedure? Did anyone from the fire department even return your phone call when your church was burning?"

Pastor Said sighed. He glanced at Yousef's empty cup, then stared past the adjacent tables of Alexandria's Grand Café. "They *still* haven't called, and it's been nearly a week. A scourge is on." The older man drummed his fingers on the table. "The Brotherhood blames Christians for their loss of power and have vowed 'bloody revenge' on us. No one is safe, Yousef."

Yousef smiled. "We may be seeing Samer sooner than we thought—but nothing will match seeing Jesus. Oh come, Lord Jesus."

After sitting quietly for several more minutes, the two men stood up, embraced, kissed each other's cheeks, and departed in opposite directions. At the entrance to the café, Yousef turned left toward the Moaz traffic circle.

He had time today to take a long walk home through the ancient city founded by Alexander the Great. Once a showcase of learning, progress, and the early church, Alexandria was now one of the darkest places in Egypt, if not the world. Even the once world-renowned Alexandrian Lighthouse was gone.

A stronghold for the Muslim Brotherhood, the city foundered. Its tourism industry had collapsed, and the remaining Christians lived discreetly—at least most Christians did. Yousef was an exception.

Today—Friday—his long way home would include a pass by the El-Mursi Abul Abbas Mosque. Yousef could not resist a prayer walk around the site on the prime day of the week for Muslim worship.

As Yousef reached the Moaz intersection, he heard shouting a block to the south, followed by the distinct sound of tear gas cans exploding. Gunshots were next. Another Brotherhood protest had turned ugly.

He stopped at the corner and scanned the traffic circle. For several minutes, he watched vehicles moving in a normal pattern and didn't notice the small crowd gathering behind him. Yousef was about to resume his walk when a hand grabbed his hair and wrenched his head backward and down, forcing him to his knees. Another hand pressed a nine-inch blade to his exposed throat.

"And what have we here? A Christian that has come to proselytize us?" The voice at his back made Yousef's flesh crawl. "We know who you are . . . Yousef! I know you from my neighborhood and that you are not a Muslim . . . yet."

Mohammad al-Hassan yanked Yousef's head sideways and

screamed in his face: "And today you will convert to Islam, or you will lose your head! Say the Shahada and worship Allah— right now!" Yousef had not recognized the voice, but the man's face was familiar. "If you don't, you will die and go straight to hell, where you belong!"

"Infidel! Death to the infidel!" Several dozen rough voices shouted encouragement to the knife-wielding man.

With his blade still touching Yousef's throat just above the Adam's apple, al-Hassan preached to the crowd: "The Hadith has instructed us with these words: 'I have been ordered to fight with the people till they say, none has the right to be worshipped but Allah.'"*

Images of his parents and siblings flitted through Yousef Mansour's thoughts. He looked skyward. Like the apostle John Mark, who had given up his life for Christ in this very city nearly two thousand years before, Yousef was more than ready to die.

"May I stand and speak?" Yousef strained to get the words out of his contorted throat.

Mohammad al-Hassan sneered. "You may say a few words before you confess your allegiance to Allah."

As Yousef stood, the knife moved with him as if attached to his throat. He lifted his right hand. "I have made my decision!"

The crowd cheered.

"Here I stand, and this is what I have decided: I will never bow to anyone other than my Savior, the Lord Jesus Christ! You

---

* Sahih al-Bukhari 4:196

can threaten me, you can torture me, and you can kill me. But I will *never* convert!"

The stunned crowd stared in silence at the man with a knife at his throat.

## A MESSAGE FROM YOUSEF

I fully expected to die that day on the street corner in Alexandria. I had resigned myself to it and was ready—but *Jesus* intervened.

Do you remember when Jesus was driven out of Nazareth after He spoke in the synagogue? He had shocked the people there with these words:

> The Spirit of the Lord is upon Me,
> Because He has anointed Me
> To preach the gospel to the poor;
> He has sent Me to heal the brokenhearted,
> To proclaim liberty to the captives
> And recovery of sight to the blind,
> To set at liberty those who are oppressed;
> To proclaim the acceptable year of the LORD.
>     (Luke 4:18–19 NKJV)

The irate crowd took Him to "the brow of the hill" intending to throw Him off a cliff (v. 29). They wanted nothing less than His death.

But a miracle happened: Jesus simply passed "through the

midst of them" (v. 30). No one resisted, and from the account in Luke 4, it is not clear exactly how this occurred. Did Jesus hold up His hand and look into their eyes so that they backed off in fear? Did they just freeze? Did Jesus become invisible?

Whatever it was must have been similar to the miracle I experienced that day at the traffic circle. When I announced to my killer and to the crowd that I would bow only to Jesus, something very strange happened to Mohammad al-Hassan.

He froze.

He stood there for more than a minute without moving a muscle. He was a statue.

While he waited—for whatever he was waiting for—I waited. The *crowd* waited. I stood with the blade at my neck, longing to see my Jesus. I was *so* close.

But it was not to be. Mohammad finally moved. He simply dropped the knife and walked away. No one in the crowd said a thing. They just followed Mohammad down the street. After another minute or so, I was alone on the sidewalk.

What an honor it would have been to become a martyr like John Mark. He died not far from where I knelt before the crowd. Ever since my dear Samer had been martyred in Cairo, I figured I would face a similar death.

So why am I here while Samer is in the presence of Jesus? I believe there are two reasons.

*First:* My mission—spreading the gospel—is not complete. In the Luke 4 passage, Jesus' mission was not complete, and His time had not yet come. He was called to die on the cross in Jerusalem, not be pushed off a cliff in Nazareth. Either way,

He was ready to die. And so was I. I had given up my life and was ready to die a violent death. I never for an instant thought I would be spared or that God would intervene. I was sure my life was over, and Jesus brought me to that moment with His confidence. Only He could have made me feel that way. But it was not to be.

Jesus' followers are being martyred all around the Middle East—and most of the world, for that matter. I have seen videos from Syria and Iraq as men and women are beheaded for their faith. That happens more than I care to think about, and let me tell you, it's a ghastly way to die.

But Jesus left me here to lift Him up in Alexandria. It's as simple as that to me. I have no other purpose.

*And second:* I believe Jesus has left me here to display *His* power. Muslim fundamentalists like Mohammad al-Hassan crave power. In their way of thinking, coercive power validates their religion. Yet, the power of the true God is something they have not experienced. They haven't seen it but need to glimpse it in order to compare it to what they *don't* have.

Mohammad saw the power of God for the first time as he waited to take my life. I have never felt the Spirit of the living God overcome me like I did as I stood to make my announcement. The words came out of my mouth with authority and confidence, and I think the force of those words paralyzed Mohammad. He saw God at work, and it frightened him.

Muslims often laugh at Christians because we turn the other cheek. Crimes are committed against us, and we do not retaliate. In their eyes, we are weak. Mohammad, though, did not see weakness during our confrontation. God had removed the fear from my heart, and Mohammad could not understand that sort of strength. My love for Jesus was so tangible and so strong that he could *feel* it. He could see I did not hate him for what he was about to do. Only my Savior could fill me to the point that I welcomed death. This was Jesus on display for him and the crowd.

Alexandria was once one of the four primary cities of our Christian faith. Jerusalem, Constantinople, Rome, and Alexandria each played major roles in early church history. Alexandria even trained men for ministry, but those days are long gone. Sadly, my city is known for being a "capital" of the Muslim Brotherhood. And that is why I think I'm still here—to bring Jesus back to this dark city.

Others shine the light in Alexandria as well, so pray for us. We are all being watched, and I know someone like Mohammad will come for me again one of these days. But do not worry for me.

I will never bow down but to Jesus.

# CHAPTER EIGHT

# THE GAZA STRIP INFILTRATORS

"ALI, I WOULD not go near your place if I were you."

Mahmoud whispered into the cell phone as he quickened his pace away from his friend's unassuming flat in downtown Gaza City. Passing the apartment on an evening walk, Mahmoud Najar had glanced through the front window at four men smashing dishes, ripping books from shelves, and breaking wooden chairs.

"The imam was there with them, and he was sitting on your couch, watching television!"

The five intruders were not thieves; they were sent by Hamas and fulfilling a mission to make life as miserable as possible for a suspected infidel. Ransacking of Ali Abdel Masih's apartment had become routine, although each subsequent raid was more violent than the one before. Soon, the imam would not have a working television to watch while his workers did their job.

Problems for the Gaza City resident started after a Hamas "neighborhood observer" spotted two twentyish men leaving Ali's apartment at three o'clock one morning. Mahmoud had been one of them, and he knew he had been seen. As a result, the trouble his friend and prayer partner was now in had been expected.

Mahmoud turned a corner and headed toward the traffic circle several blocks east. He pressed the phone against his head to hear his friend over the noise of the city.

"Mahmoud, you would not believe what I am witnessing right now as we speak. I'm at the Rafah border crossing. There's a new tunnel, and I just saw about fifteen boys come out with some nasty assault weapons they no doubt got straight from Egypt. The Brotherhood–Hamas connection is alive and well, I tell you. I don't think those boys are any more than twelve years old."

Mahmoud ignored the observation. "I wish you would cool it for a while, Ali. I'm all for sharing the gospel, but reaching out to Hamas? You're probably already on their hit list. They killed Rami Ayyad, and they will kill *you* without blinking." Mahmoud startled at the grinding of gears as a truck accelerated past him.

"You're right, Mahmoud. I *am* on their list," his friend replied. "Supposedly, ten of us are. But don't worry, I'm lying low and using a cover name. I'll be fine."

Mahmoud scanned the sidewalk in front of him. "That

doesn't convince me, Ali. They're looking for you. You need to get out of the Strip altogether."

"If that really becomes necessary, I'll make arrangements. Meanwhile, thanks for the concern, bro."

Ali paused, and Mahmoud wondered if they'd lost their connection.

"Hey, can you tell me when our new friends have left my apartment?" he asked after a moment.

"Sure, why?"

"Obviously, I can't go home again, and I need you to sneak in and grab me a few shirts and some other things I'd like to have." Ali paused again, then said, "Hey, I've got to go. Phone call from another MBB."*

Mahmoud clicked off his phone and checked the area before heading into the traffic circle. He wondered who was calling Ali.


"Hello?" Ali immediately recognized the voice that responded. "Yes, Jamal! I can meet tonight. You sound like it's urgent. Is everything all right?"

Ali Abdel Masih could have passed for a member of Hamas. If there were a poster to recruit young Gazans, his twenty-eight-year-old, olive-skinned Arab face tucked behind a close-cropped black beard would provide the ideal photo. Yet only his closest friends knew this militant-looking Jesus

---

* Muslim Background Believer

follower had spent the first twenty-two years of his life in the United States of America, the land of his birth. He even spoke flawless Arabic, with no trace of an American accent. But while Hamas lives for the death of Israel, Ali came to the Middle East to spread life to Palestinians. He was especially drawn to young Gazans who were likely headed toward a life of war with the Jewish State.

Jamal Ramadan sipped tea mixed with milk and gazed down the beach at the light of one small boat. He knew it must be near the breakwater a mile to the south, but darkness shrouded everything else for this 1:00 a.m. meeting with his spiritual mentor.

Jamal turned back toward Ali, swept his hand at the sprawling conglomeration of tents and aluminum shacks along the edge of the beach, and continued pouring his heart out to his friend and brother in Christ.

"Al-Shati is unbearable. I've spent my whole life in this refugee camp. Did you know there are nine different terrorist groups operating in the camps now? I don't think it will ever change. This is how it's been since 1948!"

Ali nodded.

Jamal stabbed his finger in the air toward the darkened slum. "Can you believe there are over seventy-five thousand people living in that place?" He plopped both hands on his head and closed his eyes. Then a half smile formed on his lips and he looked again at his friend. "What I think is even harder to believe is that a house church meets there, too, and everyone in the group is a former Muslim. Praise God. Ali, we worship *Jesus* right in the middle of one of the world's worst terrorist enclaves. Wow. If they knew about us . . ."

"It's no wonder they're so bold, with Prime Minister Haniyah leading the pack." Ali sifted sand through the fingers of his right hand. "He created quite the stir with his announcement to the world press: 'Hamas loves death for Allah more than you Israelis love life.' Can you believe he actually said that?"

"Unfortunately, I can."

Ali huffed. "A moonless night like this would make a great time for the IDF* to just take him out completely. Maybe they'll accommodate his wishes—since he loves death so much."

"Palestinians would shout for joy. Did you know Hamas has an approval rating of *less than* 15 percent? How pitiful is that? And to think I was going to join them at one time! I'm ashamed I ever considered it. Thank You, Jesus, for rescuing me."

Ali sat staring inland at the somber camp as he responded. "An Israeli strike is not out of the question tonight, you know. If we hear drones, I'm going to find us a place to hide."

Ali turned and scanned the blackness of the Mediterranean Sea. "There's something in the air tonight." He looked at Jamal. "Last night I was with Mahmoud in Deir al-Balah. During our meal with his family, we heard screams nearby and then four shots. The Hamas operatives never knew what hit them. Once the IDF pinpointed their location, it was over and done in seconds. I

---

* Israeli Defense Force

feel for their families, but if truth be told, the people of Gaza will have a parade once Hamas is gone for good."

"Yeah, that's one thing Palestinians and Israelis can agree on. Both sides want a Hamas-free Gaza."

They laughed at the thought, but the light moment was short-lived.

"Shhh." Ali held up a hand. The air above them buzzed like a mechanical hornet. "Drone!"

Ali and Jamal knew better than to run for cover. That would increase the likelihood of their being regarded as a target. They listened quietly as the overhead hum circled past the eastern perimeter of the Al-Shati refugee camp.

"Since Hamas has been in power, it's just not safe to be out at night. Ali, we used to play nighttime volleyball on the beach—but not anymore."

The two friends winced as a pair of flashes from the direction of the camp sliced the darkness in rapid succession. Two Qassam rockets erupted skyward and turned toward Ashkelon, a favorite target a dozen miles to the northeast in Israel.

Jamal squinted at the rocket trail, then turned to his companion. "Ali, I'm not sure I should do this, but . . . follow me." Jamal stood abruptly and motioned toward the camp.

After a furtive five-minute walk, Ali and Jamal stood, shoulders nearly touching, in blackness so deep they knew each other's presence only by the sound of their breathing in an enclosed place.

Jamal lit a match, and Ali's jaw dropped. With nothing to offer perspective, the tunnel in which they were standing could have stretched a few feet or several miles before dissolving in a dark hole.

"Jamal, how did you know this was here? You just denied ever joining Hamas, but is that true?"

"Of course, it's true. I didn't join them. But I live in a Gaza camp, bro. Word gets around, especially in Al-Shati. I hear conversations of the people everywhere, and let's just say that my next-door neighbor talks too much—and way too loud.

"The tunnels down south, at Rafah, are used to smuggle things *in* that you can't get anywhere in Gaza." He chuckled. "I ate at the Grand Palace Hotel the other day—you know, the one on Al-Rashid Street that overlooks the beach?"

"Yeah, I've been there."

"Anyway, I ordered a steak, and I'm telling you, it was delicious! Never tasted anything like it in Gaza. When I commented on it to the owner, he said they got the meat through one of the tunnels. I asked if they carry sides of beef in the underground passages, but he said, 'No, they don't *drag* it through tunnels. They walk whole herds of cows in from Egypt!'"

"That's a new one on me!" Ali studied the ceiling. "But, Jamal, this tunnel is on the *north* end of Gaza. We both know there's only one thing this could be used for."

"No doubt, my friend. It only has one function. It exists to funnel Hamas under the border to kill Israelis. It's a murder weapon. And that's why I brought us here. It's not to hide from tonight's Israeli drone work, Ali. I brought us down here so we could pray."

The match in Jamal's hand burned out, leaving the men in

darkness once again. Jamal lit another and continued, "We must pray for our people—the Palestinians who are trapped in this horrible mess we live in.

"I want us to pray, but I also want to tell you something. And I thought it would be safer to speak about it in the tunnel. I can't take a chance that anyone in the camp will hear me say it."

Ali nodded at his friend.

"Okay. Here it is. I'll just say it: Our Savior has taken away my hatred for Israelis." Jamal shook his head. "I want to pray for *them*, too, Ali. I don't hate them anymore. My heart is filled with the love of God for *Jews*."

Jamal looked Ali in the eye. "Do you remember how much I used to hate 'those Jewish swine'? I can't ever call them that any more. Can you believe I'm saying that I want to *pray* for them?"

Emotion washed over Ali, and tears spilled down his Arab-American cheeks. He spoke slowly.

"Jamal, I actually can believe it. You've been given a supernatural love. With all you've been through, your hatred, not your love, is what made sense. An IDF soldier killed your father, and your brother is in an Israeli prison. But only Jesus, man . . . only Jesus can do something so supernatural."

As Jamal's second match fizzled, Ali reached out to embrace his brother in Christ. The two men held each other for several seconds in the dark. Then Jamal stepped back and spoke into the lightless space. "Well, we know this has never been done in here before. So here goes: Father, we pray for the people of Israel. Make those rockets fall on empty fields tonight and foil the plans of Hamas. May these tunnels be discovered by the Israelis before any more die."

The passageway vibrated as a rumble overhead interrupted Jamal's prayer. The drone had found a target. Jamal and Ali grabbed hands in the dark and continued to pray.

"Hey, Ali, I like your blue shirt. I can see it right through your guitar. You want to explain how that happened?"

Four months after the night of prayer in the tunnel with Jamal, Ali strummed his Fender six-string with the four men he met regularly for prayer and worship in the Jabalia refugee camp. Bullets had turned the soundboard of his guitar into a slab of Swiss cheese.

"The bullet holes." Ali chuckled as he began the story. "These were a gift from an IDF soldier at the Erez Crossing last week when I was leaving Gaza to go to the West Bank. I got the usual questions, and then Aaron—I've gotten to know some of these guys—saw my guitar case and was immediately suspicious. The questions stopped and out came the robot."

"The robot?" asked Isam, a new believer in his early twenties.

"Isam, I can tell you haven't spent much time at the border. It's how they deal with suspicious packages or if the IDF thinks someone is wired to a bomb. They bring out the remote control robot, and it carries the questionable item a safe distance away. Those robots are actually pretty amazing. They can undo the clips on a suicide bomber's vest, while he has his hands in the air, then carry it away to the side of a hill, and boom! Or the soldiers open fire on the object. *That's* what they did to my guitar." Ali grinned.

Abdul—another new believer from the Jabalia refugee camp—snarled, "You didn't deserve that! Those Israelis are cruel! You saved for months to buy your guitar."

"Hey, look at me, Abdul. I *so* fit the profile. That soldier was just doing his job. The week before, someone really did try to get through Erez with a bomb in a guitar case. If I had known that, I would've left mine here. I don't hold anything against the guys who shot up my six-string. In fact, Aaron apologized to me after nothing exploded, and he realized it was just a musical instrument. He told me the story about what had happened the week before and asked, 'What could I do?' I think he was really sorry to have messed up my guitar."

Abdul nodded grudgingly.

"God used our encounter, though," Ali went on. "While he was questioning me, I told Aaron I was no longer a Muslim, and he asked, 'Is that possible?' I said, 'Yeah, man, I'm a Jesus follower now—just trying to live like He would each day. He was a man of peace, you know.'

"Aaron was pretty confused about that, of course, and wanted to talk more. He asked if I was a Christian. I told him I was, and then he asked me another question I think he had been waiting a long time to ask someone."

Ali pointed at his four friends—Abdul, Isam, Jamal, and Mahmoud—as he continued. "This is probably news to you guys, but for centuries, Jews have been targeted around the world as 'the Christ killers.' People who *claimed* to be Christians persecuted them for crucifying Jesus. You know: the Spanish Inquisition, the Crusades; even *Nazis* claimed to be Christians. So anyway, this Jewish IDF soldier leaned into me and nearly growled the question in my face: 'So who killed Jesus?'

"He expected me to say, 'The Jews did it,' but I prayed silently about how to respond, and even I was surprised by how perfect my answer was. '*I* killed him,' I said. 'My sins put Him on the cross.'

"The guy was speechless. He didn't say a word, and I really think the Holy Spirit pierced his heart when I said that. He felt the sincerity—and lack of bitterness—in my answer. For a Palestinian to show that he cares for an Israeli soldier? He had trouble processing that one.

"So then I hugged him and told him he has a tough job and that I would be praying for him. He just looked at me, speechless again." Ali tapped the fingers of his right hand on his own chest and said, "I can't wait to see him again."

The five men sat in silence for several seconds before Ali continued.

"And unfortunately, that may be soon. I have some bad news: I've been ordered to leave Gaza. After six years here, I've been contacted by the American consulate and been told that I must go. With Hamas in power, no Americans are allowed to stay here any longer. I'll do everything I can to come back. I even plan on getting a lawyer to fight this. But for now, I must go."

Four young disciples who now loved Jesus and who had been delivered from the hopelessness of life under Hamas looked sadly at their mentor. If Ali had never come to Gaza, each of them would likely be living the life of a terrorist—always afraid, always suppressing his own fear by inflicting greater fear on others. Ali had nurtured them in their faith. Now they would have to do that for each other.

Jamal had been silent throughout the story of the guitar and the interchange that followed. In the quiet, Ali watched Jamal study the floor, deep in thought. After a full minute, Jamal scratched his chin absent-mindedly and looked up at Ali Abdel Masih.

"I want you to baptize me, Ali. This is normal for believers, right?"

Ali nodded.

"I'm not sure what I've been waiting for." Jamal shook his head. "But I've been reading the book of Acts, and Peter baptized new believers in Caesarea, just up the coast from here. I'm not ashamed of my faith, and I'm not afraid. I want to be baptized in the Mediterranean—tonight! If we get killed, we get killed."

Ali took a deep breath and smiled at Jamal. He looked each of the other three men in the eye. "If anyone else wants to join us at the beach, let's meet behind the Al Salam Restaurant at 1:00 a.m. Just remember," he added somberly, "if Hamas sees us, we'll probably go to heaven while we're still wet."

Isam hopped down a sandy bank along the Gaza breakwater and headed up the beach toward the Al Salam Restaurant. Four other men stood at a point several hundred feet away where the beach narrows at the south side of the restaurant. Jamal had chosen the night for his baptism well. The moon was absent, leaving the beachfront dark enough so that only the night vision of an Israeli drone could have seen them easily. The only sound came from the gentle surf.

Careful never to meet in the same place twice, Ali had also chosen this *location* well. Here, the beach was fewer than fifty feet wide from sand bank to surf, so the abbreviated open space would make it even less likely they would be seen by anyone on land.

Isam arrived last, precisely at one o'clock. He joined Jamal, Mahmoud, Abdul, and Ali in silent prayer. Several minutes had passed when Ali opened his eyes and looked at the four men he had poured his life into for the past two years. They would soon find out that, tomorrow, God's work in Gaza would be in their hands.

"Amen, brothers." Ali spoke the words softly and motioned with his finger toward the water.

Five men walked quickly into the waves until they were waist deep. Ali placed his right hand over Jamal's hands, which were folded across his chest. Then, he placed his left hand between Jamal's shoulder blades and pressed gently with his right, pushing the young convert into the water.

"I baptize you, my brother, in the name of the Father, of the Son, and of the Holy Spirit."

He repeated the pattern with each of the other three men. Then, wordlessly, all five left the beach as they had arrived, departing individually in different directions.

An hour later, Jamal, Abdul, Mahmoud, Isam, and Ali had

gathered again. This time, they sat in a circle on the dirt floor of Abdul's home in the Jabalia refugee camp. Even at 2:00 a.m., eyes peeked occasionally through cracks in the tin-sided shack, and each time the eyes appeared, the group changed the subject of conversation to their favorite football team, Real Madrid.

When yet another set of eyes had gone, Abdul shared a deep concern. "I think my relatives suspect something. I'm almost positive I heard someone say the word 'converted' yesterday. We must whisper here."

"Yes." Ali spoke softly and added with a sigh, "That makes it even more difficult to tell you why I wanted to meet yet again tonight." He scanned the four faces looking at him. "Tomorrow, I must leave."

Four pairs of eyes widened.

"I received another phone call this afternoon, after we met. It was from the consulate, and I'm required to go."

Jamal closed his eyes and rubbed his forehead. The other three men simply stared at Ali.

"The ministry is now in your hands. Each of you lives in a different refugee camp—that was planned, of course. So we have Jabalia, Al-Shati, Deir al-Balah, and Al Bureji covered, but there are still four other camps without the light of the gospel. I'm praying that each of you will disciple a new believer who begins a group in each of the other camps."

He leaned toward the four listeners and continued quietly. "Each of us had different paths, but we were all Muslims desperately needing to break free from our chains when we came to follow Jesus. *He* is the One who pulled you out of Islam, not me.

At first, you were terrified of sharing your faith with Muslims, and now look at you! You're embedded in refugee camps controlled by Muslim fanatics. Mahmoud, you used to be so afraid for *me* that you were always trying to talk me out of sharing Jesus with Muslims. And today? You're the one risking your neck for Jesus. He has made you fearless and wise."

Ali paused and glanced at the floor. He raised his hands, palms up, and spoke to his small audience. "Why was I born in America and each of you in Gaza? I can't understand all of that, but now our lives have direction. Jesus replaced the disgust we felt for Islam, when we first came to Him, with compassion and an unquenchable desire to make Him known to Muslims. At one time, you supported global jihad and were headed for Hamas, Islamic Jihad, or ISIS. Now *they* are our mission field."

The four hearers nodded solemnly.

"Brothers, terrorists need Jesus." Ali pointed at Jamal, Abdul, Isam, and Mahmoud in turn. "Stay strong together. A great persecution is on the way. I think we all know Hamas is really in this fight for money and political power. Their leaders get rich by positioning themselves as the great 'Zionist destroyers.' All the while, upper-level leaders buy mansions on the beach. They pull out their Islamic faith and dust it off only when it's expedient for them.

"But: *watch out for the Salafis.*[*] They're the *real* fanatics. Islamic Jihad is formidable, too. We're like the Israelites in the Old Testament. Our enemies surround us, much as the ones who

---

* A strict, traditionalist sect of Islam.

tried to take David's life in Psalm 52: 'You who practice deceit,' he quoted, 'your tongue plots destruction, it is like a sharpened razor. You love evil rather than good.' But we? We 'are like a green olive tree in the house of God'" (vv. 2–3, 8).

Ali leaned back, pressed his hands together, and touched his fingers to his lips. "When you see an olive tree, remember that. It's a promise God made to the Israelites before they entered the land, and it's a promise for us, too. The olive tree has always been here, and it symbolizes *faithfulness*. Olive trees in Gaza come from a root system that is well over a thousand years old—maybe even two thousand. They are virtually indestructible. And so are *you*. Until it's your time to be with Jesus, you are bulletproof."

The group leader paused to let his words soak in.

"And one more thing: if an olive branch is cut off from the tree, you can replant the branch months later, and it will grow again." Once more, he pointed to each in turn. "If you get separated from one other, remember: it's not over. God will bring you together again—in this life or the next."

The five men, still seated in a circle, placed hands on each other's shoulders and prayed. One by one, starting with Jamal, they broke into tears. Jamal, Abdul, Isam, and Mahmoud knew they all shared the same thought: would they ever see Ali again?

By noon the next day, Ali was sipping coffee in a café at Yad Mordecai on the Israel side of the border with Gaza. Although he had looked for Aaron at the Erez Crossing facility and couldn't find him, he added to his Israeli connections as soon as he reached the little restaurant.

From among the IDF dining there, Ali had befriended three soldiers. He charmed the small group with stories about life in Gaza, and the newcomer further captivated them when he described his early life as a Muslim extremist. As Aaron had been, the three soldiers were shocked to hear Ali recount how *Jesus* had transformed him. The meeting went well.

For the next four years, Ali continued to mentor Jamal, Abdul, Isam, and Mahmoud through the Internet and on the phone. He encouraged them by reading Scripture and praying. The disciples also shared with Ali their own versions of the misery of life in Gaza. Now that Hamas was the official government of the Strip, the four men wondered if they would ever see the world outside of their six-mile-wide, twenty-five-mile-long prison.

As Gaza sank to new lows under the corrupt dominion of Hamas, Jamal, Mahmoud, Abdul, and Isam prepared themselves for the new persecution that was undoubtedly coming soon. Typical in the long history of oppression, a single event triggered the outbreak they feared: two Hamas observers spotted a late-night baptism on the Gaza Beach.

The next morning, Jamal Ramadan found himself in a meeting—but not one he had arranged. He was about to be beaten senseless in a grungy shack at the center of the Al-Shati Refugee Camp.

A twentysomething bearded man with a sweat-drenched face bent to eye level with Jamal, who was kneeling on the floor, and screamed, "What are the names of the men doing the baptism last night?" The volume was intended not only for its effect on Jamal but also to broadcast a message to anyone within earshot of the hut. Jamal said nothing.

"You are a filthy, Zionist spy," the man continued, "and you will pay for this! Your family will die, but not until we are through torturing you."

The shouting man stood straight and scanned the three others in the room who were nodding approval. Then he screamed again at Jamal, "This is your last chance! Christianity is a religion for losers! Islam will dominate the world! We see it now, and you will see it soon—if you live long enough. Renounce Jesus Christ!"

Jamal raised his eyes, smiled gently at his accuser, and whispered his answer: "No way."

One of the Hamas thugs pulled a homemade whip from the strap behind his back. "If you love Jesus so much, then you will be beaten like Him! We'll continue our interrogation with forty lashes."

Jamal grimaced under the first lash.

After forty, he moaned softly but kept his composure.


Across town, Abdul dove out the front door and landed facedown in the busy street as his uncle fired a second shot. The first had grazed his left ear as he sat on the floor of his ramshackle house in Jabalia. Fearing a third shot, he rolled behind a donkey cart parked a few feet away, then hopped to his feet and zig-zagged down the street toward the Salah al-Din Road. Perhaps his uncle wouldn't fire again down a crowded street. As Abdul raced around a building at the corner, he hit number 2 on his speed dial.

"Mahmoud! I'm headed your way! Are you in Deir al-Balah? My father sent his brother to kill me this morning. He's with Islamic Jihad, and I should have seen this coming." Abdul described the attack and the two near-miss gunshots. "I can't go back home!"

"I'm here and waiting for you, brother. I'm worried about Jamal, though. He calls me every morning to pray before we begin our prayer walk through the camp. He never misses, but today he did. I was planning to go to Al-Shati, but I think something is happening with Jamal. We need to fast until we hear from him."

"I tried to call Jamal, too, Mahmoud. I got no answer, so I called his brother. He sounded strange on the phone, and I just don't trust him. First he asked me to tell him where I was. Then he asked if I wanted to come to Al-Shati to wait for Jamal. He's up to no good. I also think I heard laughing in the back-ground—and I doubt they were telling jokes. We need to stick together. Can you contact Isam?"

"Yes, I'll call him after we hang up."

Abdul checked over his shoulder to see if he was being fol-lowed. "Mahmoud, I'm compromised with my family, Jamal can't be found, and things in Gaza are out of control. I think we better brace ourselves: a ground war is coming to Gaza soon. The killing of the three yeshiva boys started the ball rolling.

Then the Arab child was found murdered. Next came Arab riots all over Israel, and then the endless barrage of Hamas rockets. IDF air strikes are not stopping Hamas, and I wonder how long Israel will let this go before they send in troops and level Gaza."

"I wonder, too, Mahmoud. But let's figure out what's happening to *us* right now."

"Right. I'll call Isam."

Isam winced as he picked up his cell phone from the bedside table. "Hi, friend."

"Isam, are you safe? Jamal is missing, and Abdul and I are afraid he's been killed. Abdul had a close call just now. His uncle shot twice at him from point-blank range, but the Lord, I believe, redirected the bullets. He's meeting me here at Deir al-Balah; Jabalia is off-limits for him now."

Isam replied weakly, "Actually, I'm in the hospital, Mahmoud. This morning, I went out to grab some bread for breakfast, and on my way back to Al Bureji, a gang jumped me. They beat me up pretty bad and stabbed me three times. Six of them recited infidel suras over me. It was Abu Bakir al-Ansari's group—Salafi militants. There was no way I could get free. Mahmoud, I thought I was dead. I closed my eyes and committed my life into Jesus' hands."

Isam paused, holding back emotion. "You remember what Ali told us about being bulletproof until God decides our time is up?"

"Yes," Mahmoud responded thoughtfully, "I remember."

"As suddenly as they had jumped me, every one of those guys ran off. They just *left*! Did God send angels? They had to be frightened by someone or something." Isam choked on his words and whispered, "I witnessed a miracle today."

Mahmoud whistled through his teeth. "Wow."

"If we ever had any doubt that God wants us in Gaza, I think it's gone now." Isam continued, energy building as he spoke. "Look at what's happened to all of us in just the last few hours. Ali warned us that a great persecution is coming." Isam looked at his phone. "Mahmoud, what happened to you?"

"Ha! Nothing! I had a headache last night and thought that was pretty bad."

"Mahmoud," Isam laughed, "are you sure you're walking with Jesus? A *headache*?"

"I know; how lame is that, right?" Mahmoud chuckled, then added, "Hey, I'm going to get Abdul on the line so we can pray together for Jamal."

Isam listened as Mahmoud made the connection and Abdul's voice came on the line. The three prayed for Jamal, pleading that the Lord would preserve his life.


*I want to die.*

Jamal awoke the morning after the first beating, his back in agony. He did not know that worse lay in store. Salafi jihadists waited their turns to beat the infidel, and he would endure six more days of torture.

During the same week, Mahmoud, Isam, and Abdul fasted and prayed, hoping for word from Jamal. Isam endured his own torture, a pain-filled walk from the hospital to meet Mahmoud and Abdul at a prearranged spot in downtown Gaza City. The vacant, bombed-out building became their new residence and hiding place.

On a Thursday night, day three of their seclusion, Gaza imploded. Israeli gunboats pounded the southern end of the Strip while tanks rolled into the north. IDF troops stormed the rogue state, gunning for an engagement that would allow them to destroy Hamas.

In the fracas, Jamal's captors left him unguarded and the badly damaged believer limped out of his torture chamber. He squinted to protect his eyes from blinding flashes as rapid-fire explosions glared across the Gaza skyline. Too weak to travel far, Jamal found an alley and tucked himself under a pile of rubble to spend the night.

On Friday morning, Mahmoud woke up before Abdul and Isam.

"Hey guys." He tapped the other men on their shoulders. "It's snowing."

"Mahmoud," Abdul grumbled, yawning, "quit trying to be funny. I'm tired."

"Well, it looks like snow! I think the IDF is trying to tell us something. They're dropping leaflets."

Several printed slips of paper fluttered through what was left of a wall. Mahmoud grabbed one. The message was written in Arabic.

"Listen to this, guys. 'For the citizens of Gaza: For your own safety, avoid being present in the vicinity of Hamas operatives and facilities, and those of other terror organizations, beginning at 10 a.m. today.'" Mahmoud held the paper toward his friends. "It's time to find a safer place, brothers."

As Abdul and Isam sat up on the cement floor and stretched, Mahmoud's cell phone buzzed.

"Hmmm. I don't recognize this number." Mahmoud pondered his phone, wondering if he should answer, then touched it to accept the call. His mouth gaped as he recognized the voice on the phone. "Jamal! Thank God you're alive!"

Mahmoud tapped his phone, and Jamal's voice sounded from the speaker. He sounded weak, and the three men huddled close to hear him.

Isam whispered, "Jesus, thank You."

After Jamal's initial greeting, Abdul couldn't contain himself, hopped up, and started jumping around the room. His enthusiasm waned, though, as Jamal described his torture and escape.

"I was whipped, beaten with two-by-fours, and burned with lighters. I haven't eaten in a week. They were after your names, but I never gave you up. Jesus sustained me." Jamal choked on the words. "I cried out for Him to take me home, but when the IDF entered Gaza, the people of Al-Shati started running. I simply walked out of the place they had been holding me, and no one said a word."

"Where are you now?" Mahmoud almost hollered in his excitement.

"I'm in Gaza City. Early this morning, a total stranger looked at me and thought I had been in a fight against the Israelis. He let me shower at his apartment and then bandaged me up.

"I need a day or two to rest. My body is one big bruise." Jamal paused, choosing his next words. "While I was being held, I believe God showed me something. The people of Gaza are desperate. This physical war is a reflection of the spiritual war raging in the heavenlies above us. Jesus put us here—all four of us—for this time . . . Where can we meet and make a plan? I have some ideas to share."

The four Gaza disciples discovered a remarkable opportunity in Operation Protective Edge, Israel's initiative to control Hamas. Jamal, Mahmoud, Abdul, and Isam began their own operation to bring the Kingdom of God to Gaza City and the northern refugee camps. They prayed with people, passed out food and water to the displaced, and found occasions to discreetly shine Jesus' light into the darkness.

The IDF bombings were constant and unpredictable, and their force and volume left Gaza residents badly shaken. The devastation of war and the atrocities of Hamas offered many openings for compassion. Hamas routinely shot Palestinians who fled from buildings Israel was about to bomb. Warning leaflets provided advance notice of places Hamas could use as death traps for civilians whose demise could then be used in the public relations war against Israel.

Jamal, Mahmoud, Abdul, and Isam established their new base in a mostly destroyed building a block from the Al-Shifa Hospital in central Gaza City. But when a rumor hit the streets that a bunker had been built to hide rockets and launchers under the hospital, the four moved on to another barely standing building several blocks farther away.

Almost nonstop gunfire and IDF missile strikes robbed them of sleep every night. Two hours of sound sleep became a luxury. Yet the four put their awake time to good use. They prayed together most of each night. Swarms of uprooted people meant they were no longer alone in the building, but the believing foursome cried out fearlessly to Jesus, even though they knew others were listening. Gazans were people without hope, but hearing the passionate prayers brought a sense of calm.

The men prayed for Palestinian believers—both the few in above-ground churches and the former Muslims who met underground. They prayed for Christian brothers and sisters in the IDF (they knew of some!) and for their safety. But when it came to Hamas and the other Islamic terrorist groups, the four men prayed a pointed and specific prayer: "Lord save them, take them from power, *or strike them dead.*"

Although the IDF ground assault appeared to have no effect on Hamas's rocket launches, the battle raged as rank-and-file terrorists were targeted and systematically destroyed. Hamas' upper leadership was rumored to be safely hiding somewhere outside of Gaza, and yet their demonic rule continued. Hamas operatives dragged innocent Palestinian citizens into terrorist enclaves to ensure their deaths by Israeli attacks, and although the rest of the world talked of "peace in the Middle East," Gazans expected only more truces shattered by a flurry of rockets. Would peace ever become a reality and not just talk?

A month into Operation Protective Edge, peace did arrive— at least for Mahmoud Najar.

## A MESSAGE FROM ALI

Our dear Mahmoud went to be with Jesus much sooner than we had hoped, and we still don't know the exact source of the explosion that killed him. Was it an Israeli strike? Or did a Hamas rocket explode before launching? We may never know this side of heaven.

We do know Mahmoud departed the evil, the turmoil, the heartache, and the hopelessness of Gaza for a much better place. He may not have been a martyr in the same way some have been, but he was walking into Deir al-Balah refugee camp on his last day to share Jesus there. Then he was gone.

Even though all is well with Mahmoud, it is not well in Gaza. At one time, the Strip represented everything I most detest about Islam. From the outside, the camps appear as Muslim ghettos manipulated by jihadists to support and spread their fanaticism. Inside, though, it is different, and I learned that Jesus can be seen in astounding ways in the worst of situations.

*Real* people live in refugee camps—people created in the image of God. For decades, their lives have been nothing short of miserable, and seeing the circumstances firsthand, I came to believe the conflict there is unsolvable in human terms. Political solutions never address spiritual problems.

Israelis and Palestinians are at an impasse. Israelis deserve a secure state. Palestinians need real homes. Israeli children near Gaza often have school in bomb shelters. Muslim fanatics use Palestinians to terrorize the Jewish State. Palestinians live in pitiful conditions in the refugee camps.

The extremists' hatred for Israel knows no limits, and yet they care nothing about the people of Gaza, either. They consider them pawns. So many people are killed in Gaza needlessly! I also think Israel does not get the credit it deserves for long-suffering. The continual Hamas rocket assaults leave Israelis in Ashdod, Ashkelon, and Sderot in panic mode. When the IDF finally responds after *many* Hamas attacks, I must say it is usually not "an eye for an eye" but rather "an eye for a thousand eyes." But then, war is never fair.

Gaza and West Bank Palestinians feel rejected by the world. I've heard it said that the oil sales from just *one day* in Saudi Arabia would be enough to build a home for every Palestinian in Israel and the rest of the Middle East. But don't expect the Saudi Kingdom to ever write *that* check.

God, though, has room in His heart to love both Palestinians and Jews. Jesus is the ultimate solution. Only He can heal the human hurt and win the spiritual war. Jamal, Abdul, Isam, and Mahmoud show what can become of people when Jesus delivers them. He filled their hearts with love for Arabs *and* Jews.

For the rest of us? Pray for Palestinians. Pray for Jews. And pray that God will open a door for me to return to the world's largest prison, one that has captured my heart forever: the Gaza Strip.

# CONCLUSION

WHEN PETER AND John became the first followers of the Way to be thrown in prison, they rejoiced that "they had been counted worthy of suffering disgrace for the Name" (Acts 5:41). The persecuted believers of today—the new face of Christianity—have that same spirit, and they want to say something to you: "don't feel sorry for us."

Getting sympathy is not why they wanted their stories to be told. Their lives are full and overflowing with purpose. Their joy is refreshing. They have embraced the danger and the high calling they've been given. Their trials are not random. As I said in the introduction, a reason for all of this is that *Jesus' message of love and reconciliation thrives in a climate where hostility, danger, and martyrdom are present.*

The threat of hostility, danger, and martyrdom are not

realistic options for those of us who become followers of Jesus in the West. But for people in the Middle East and other parts of the world, Christianity is synonymous with a life of extreme danger. Yet even though personal hostility, danger, and martyrdom may not be present in your life, there is something else you are experiencing: *you are suffering.* Did you know that?

Paul, in his earlier life, dished out persecution but he finished his life on the receiving end of it. Other than Jesus Himself, Paul is the New Testament portrait of persecution. In 1 Corinthians, he tells us "if one member suffers, all the members suffer" (12:26 NKJV).

Your connection to those living in persecution is stronger than you may think—if one suffers, we all suffer. That is why you recently may have felt unsettled, angry, or somewhat disoriented by the pervasive evil in the world and overwhelmed at the bombardment of Christians globally as you view it on television or read about it online or in print media.

You *should* feel this way. After all, this is an attack on your family. And, of course, ultimately, it's an attack on Jesus.

## SO WHAT'S NEXT?

Your journey to the underground is now complete—at least the first phase of it. You see, the stories are still being written. And now it's time for you to step into the narrative. Your family needs you, perhaps now more than ever.

Maybe you won't be called to endure the refining fire of

persecution, but you are called to walk alongside of those who are. Here are a few ways you can continue your walk and stay connected with your underground family.

## ANSWER THESE TWO QUESTIONS

In chapter 1 of my previous book, *Dreams and Visions: Is Jesus Awakening the Muslim World?*, Kamal Assam, an Egyptian follower of Christ, asked Noor, a committed Muslim and mother of eight children who was having Jesus dreams, two questions that had to be answered. Noor passionately wanted to follow Jesus, but Kamal had to make sure she knew what she was getting into before she committed her life to Him. So Kamal asked the following:

- Are you willing to suffer for Jesus?
- Are you willing to die for Jesus?

I believe these same two questions are foundational for everyone who follows Jesus today, no matter where they currently reside on the planet. As I write this, I find myself wondering how we Christians ever thought serving Christ could demand anything less than this kind of a commitment? How could I have missed these essentials and think they were for some believers but certainly not me?

Once you have settled the questions in your heart, though, all other trials in life pale in comparison. If the questions are not settled for you, could this be the reason you are experiencing frustration and feel stale in your faith?

Jesus said, "Whoever does not take up their cross and follow me is not worthy of me" (Matt. 10:38). Somehow when I read those words from Matthew the first time, I thought, *Wow, look at what those disciples and first century believers had to go through! They had to be willing to die on a cross. I'm glad those days are over!*

Wrong! These diagnostic questions are for all believers until Jesus returns. Did I think just because I live in America that I would never be faced with the possibility of dying for my faith? Because we have the strongest military in the world, that option was off the table?

No, friend, that option has always been *on* the table—whether we knew it or not. So before you finish reading, it's probably time to settle this in your soul, once and for all. Take some time to let God search your heart. Then answer:

- Am I willing to suffer for Jesus?
- Am I willing to die for Jesus?

For you as a believer—if you answer "yes" to the two questions—this is a spiritual game changer. Everything will be different now.

## THEY'VE BLESSED YOU; NOW BLESS THEM

From now until Jesus returns, persecution will increase and so will martyrdom. You've just been introduced to—and we hope inspired by—your brothers and sisters who live in danger.

Now you can do something for them.

Your prayers are vital to those who live on the front lines. But have you ever noticed that life gets busy and good intentions can take a nosedive off your priority list and never return? That's the reason for 8thirty8. A growing number of believers are tuned in and connected to the underground daily, and to join them, all you need is an alarm and access to the Internet.

The 8thirty8 challenge calls you to specific prayer for brothers and sisters in danger. Here's what you do: set your watch or phone to 8:38 p.m., and when the alarm goes off, pray for those who, because of their faith in Christ, are in prison, persecution, or danger. And to make sure your prayers are up-to-the-minute current, strategic, and not the anemic Lord-bless-everyone-in-danger kind of prayers, link to www.facebook.com/8thirty8 to keep up with specific needs.

The page posts daily, SOS prayer alerts for Jesus followers worldwide, and you will often find that you can pray for brothers and sisters in prison, persecution, and danger before the story even hits news outlets (if it ever does). And that's the way we think it should be: Jesus' family praying as the *first response*.

Through 8thirty8 you will even be able to send prayers and connect personally with your brothers and sisters under fire. We use cover names to insure their security, just like we did in this book, but you will connect directly to them. After all, you're family, and it's time for you to meet each other.

And where did the 8thirty8 come from? God birthed this prayer movement in Jerusalem during a Hamas rocket attack. I had just received confirmation from various national leaders that churches were burning to the ground in Egypt; Christians were being nailed to crosses in Syria; and a dear pastor friend was sentenced to more time in a Tehran prison. My heart was heavy, but God calmed it by calling me to pray and to recite Romans 8:38–39—and from Jerusalem, a prayer movement for the persecuted church spread like a fire.

The verses are the heart of Romans 8, which is the New Testament "landing page" for believers suffering:

> For I am convinced that neither death nor life, neither angels nor demons, neither the present nor the future, nor any powers, neither height nor depth, nor anything else in all creation, will be able to separate us from the love of God that is in Christ Jesus our Lord. (vv. 38–39)

At 8:38 p.m. when your alarm goes off, just stop what you are doing for a moment, and pray for the family of Christ around the world who are in prison, persecution, and danger. The timing is significant. As nighttime falls on us in the West, daytime is just beginning in the Middle East, North Africa, and Asia. And what will they face today? It could be persecution or maybe even death. By praying each evening, you send believers there into the day with a prayer of blessing and hope—and with the promise found in Romans. Stand with your family.

As my wife, JoAnn, and I travel throughout the Middle East, Africa, and Asia, saints of God tell us how overwhelmed with gratitude they are that their family in the West daily remembers them in prayer. They often say, "We send out love to our brothers and sisters in America and pray for them daily. How can we pray more specifically?"

And then we cry. *They are praying for us?* Astounding.

## A FINAL QUESTION

As we began our journey, I raised a question about Christianity: are we winning or losing? I had to ask this since most people take their worldview from cable news or Internet stories. But now that you've traveled up to the front lines of the raging spiritual battle in our world today and have an insider's view, what would you conclude?

Jesus had an answer: "Do not be afraid of those who kill the body but cannot kill the soul" (Matt. 10:28).

Paul also knew this and wrote: "Who shall separate us from the love of Christ? Shall trouble or hardship or persecution or famine or nakedness or danger or sword? . . . No, in all things we are more than conquerors" (Rom. 8:35, 37).

And Christians stand on those truths today—whether they face prison, persecution, danger, or even death. Their collective cry is: "We are not afraid!"

So in all of this Jesus wins. To Him belongs 100 percent of the glory. And for all of us who follow Him, how can we call this anything but one of our finest hours?

Yes. We are winning.

# ABOUT THE AUTHORS

TOM DOYLE pastored churches in Colorado, Texas, and New Mexico for twenty years, and his involvement in the Middle East began with leading Bible Tours to Israel, Jordan, and Egypt. He eventually became a licensed tour guide in Israel. Along the way, Tom and his wife JoAnn fell in love with the people and soon it became clear that God was calling them to do something risky—to get involved. They jumped into working full-time in the Middle East just a few months before 9/11—a game-changing event for America and the Middle East. Tom now serves as the Vice President and Middle East Director of e3 Partners, a global church planting ministry. JoAnn is also with e3, and leads Not Forgotten, which is e3's Middle East women's initiative. Tom is the author of seven books, including *Dreams and Visions: Is Jesus Awakening the Muslim World?* The Doyles have six children and four grandchildren, and hopefully many more on the way!

GREG WEBSTER is co-founder of New Vantage Publishing Partners, a book development and marketing firm, and creative director of Webster Creative Group. The collaborator of more than a dozen books for a variety of authors, including Tom Doyle's previous book *Dreams and Visions*, he holds an MA in theology from Fuller Theological Seminary and a BA in journalism and an MBA from the University of Georgia. He lives and works in rural Tennessee, just outside Nashville, with his wife of thirty-four years and the six of his eight children who have not yet left the nest.

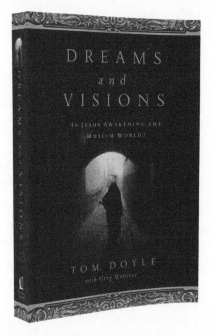